THE MACHIAVELLIANS

THE MACHIAVELLIANS

A Social Psychological Study of Moral Character and Organizational Milieu

by

STANLEY S. GUTERMAN

UNIVERSITY OF NEBRASKA PRESS · LINCOLN

Standard Book Number 8032–0707–7
Library of Congress Catalog Card Number: 69–19104

Manufactured in the United States of America

Contents

Foreword

As sociologists have become part of the academic establishment, directing large projects, seeing their work appear in public discussions and even in Supreme Court briefs, or being invited to Washington as consultants, they have also become the target of harsh criticism. The attacks are varied. Men in the hard sciences sneer at their scientific pretensions. Humanists and reformers, perhaps their most indefatigable critics, are more likely to assault them for being dehumanized, too little engaged with live issues, and unwilling to expose the corruption of an ugly society.

The dedicated sociologist is thus likely to be pulled in opposing directions. Admiring the apparent elegance of the physical sciences, he would like to divest himself of his native and naïve prejudices and to create precise measuring instruments for analyzing objectively this curious system, the human society. However, he is also likely to have been attracted to the field because of his keen interest in human beings and their exasperating or tragic problems. He is likely to be politically a reformer, and morally indignant. Thus, within the devoted sociologist will be found both a scientist and a reformer, struggling for expression.

Some sociologists stifle the scientist, and others force the reformer to remain mute. Other solutions can also be observed, such as dividing one's time between objective analyses and participating in reform groups, or writing both cool analyses for professional journals and philosophical or moralistic articles for more popular media.

In this monograph, the author has pursued yet another path, analytic exploration of a peculiarly moral phenomenon, the extent to which people decide and act in a Machiavellian fashion. By ascertaining the kinds of settings that generate a higher or lower degree of Machiavellianism, he contributes to our understanding of a personality variable that without a doubt plays a considerable role in all our lives.

I myself deplore the label, since Machiavelli deserves more praise than he gets. If princes of his day had in fact followed his advice, they would undoubtedly have enjoyed longer reigns, and their subjects would have been more contented. Nevertheless, the social psychologists who developed the various forms of the "Mach scale" were correct in part, since Machiavelli did implicitly urge that the wise ruler take stock of his situation, rationally calculate his own advantages, manipulate people for his own best ends, and not hesitate to use force or fraud if the profit were high enough. Thus, the person who ranks high on a scale of Machiavellianism will treat others as pawns, as things, and will feel less bound than others to the moral beliefs of his group.

This study, then, relates a psychological variable to a set of social structures, a task that is both fruitful and beset with difficulties. In our cocktail analyses, we are likely to "explain" others' behavior by bringing forth some psychological trait—"she is masochistic"; "he is attached to his mother"; or "he seems aggressive, but he is really shy." We are likely to forget that we know many others who have similar traits, but who have *behaved* differently. Unfortunately, a single trait explains only part of the behavior. We are also unlikely to explore carefully the *social structure* that generates more or less of such a trait. Guterman's analysis deals with both of these problems—the variables other than Machiavellianism that affect behavior, and the social variables that are correlated with this psychological pattern.

Although studies of Machiavellianism are indeed of recent vintage, the reader will also discover that the author has traced their theoretical underpinnings to some of the great classics, by Freud, Cooley, and Toennies. Of course, the ramifications of this inquiry go much further than the space permitted to the author. For example, if we can state some of the social factors that generate a manipulative, amoral attitude, will they also explain the personality that is hag-ridden by his superego, driven by his fear of doing wrong? Every sociologist has at some point considered the importance of the individual's commitment to group values, but it seems obvious that the members of a group must also behave rationally and not blindly follow a rule learned in childhood. What is the optimum balance between accepting the discipline of ethical rules as they are handed down and a rational calculation of advantage?

Guterman also raises a host of questions that are in part moral and in part sociological, but lead beyond the task he has focused on. First, of course, is the question of *whose* morals are we to follow? For most of us are self-appointed prophets at times, or moral prigs. Second, everyone is bombarded with a host of conflicting role definitions from others, and to an astonishing degree we accept many ethical rules that are in opposition. The moral code that is enjoined on the physician may conflict with part of his code as a father, or friend, or professor in a university. We are reared and controlled by many groups, and the moral rules we accept are a jumble.

It is within that kind of quandary that the temptation to behave in a Machiavellian fashion arises; and, as Guterman shows, the kinds of settings that are most like the modern moral jumble are also likely to increase the personality trait of Machiavellianism.

By asking us to consider the importance of this trait, the author is also raising a number of issues without being able to deal with all of them. For example, the study of the interaction between personality and social traits requires that we ask once more whether a given psychological characteristic is indeed properly to be viewed only as a personality variable, or whether it might profitably be analyzed as a *social* trait. In what sense is Machiavellianism part of the personality structure or, instead, a common mode of social behavior that will appear or become widespread under certain types of social pressures? For example, if a group or population segment such as Negroes, children, or the Walloons believe they are treated as pawns, as things, is it not likely that they, in turn, will respond with Machiavellian calculations and behavior?

Similarly, the gossip that has been handed down to us from Renaissance Florence suggests that, in that exciting but tension-ridden period, many people exhibited this kind of behavior. Can we simply assume that their personalities were Machiavellian, or is it a more parsimonious hypothesis to assert that their social structure generated more Machiavellian behavior?

To ask such questions is to clarify an important moral point. It is not wise to assume that all Machiavellian behavior nor all such personalities are "bad," to be condemned. Correspondingly, even when we are morally indignant at being oppressed, we cannot assume that a Machiavellian has imposed his will upon us. Doubtless at various phases in the history of any group a Machiavellian leader or policy will contribute to its survival, and even to the larger society. Faced with dangerous enemies, even the most idealistic group needs to treat them as objects rather than as ends in themselves.

Correspondingly, it is not only the Machiavellians who have contributed to the evil and hurt of human existence. One might indeed mount a strong argument that we can at least buy them off, bribe them, or convince them it would be too unprofitable to damage or oppress us. However, the true believer, the ardently committed leader, may wish to alter our desires and our lives beyond recognition—for our own good or that of the society. On a less grand scale, the policeman who protects his colleague in uniform by falsely swearing no brutality was committed; the physician who refuses to condemn his fellow surgeon after an incompetent operation; or the busybody who publicizes the sins of his neighbor, may all be hurting others with the highest of selfless motives.

Thus, to examine the phenomenon of Machiavellianism is to focus upon only one thread of a complex fabric. However, it is an important one, and the more significant because of the related problems it raises. A final issue is worth noting, although it goes beyond the content of this book. By examining both the processes that generate Machiavellianism and some of its consequences, Guterman has directed our attention to a wider range of social phenomena that people believe are important, but which are given scant attention in contemporary sociology. Machiavellianism is one of these. Within recent years, a few analysts have come to believe that "trust" is not simply a moral term, but is an important social process that needs to be studied empirically in many areas of social interaction. Similarly, the concept of "justice" may be analyzed morally, but without question we have failed to explore a fundamental empirical matter if we have not also asked whether the members of a society or subgroup believe they suffer injustice.

In short, an analysis of the central daily *concerns* of human beings may lead us to some of the powerful forces in social action. We need not, as Guterman does not, confine our observation and study to the limits of common-sense notions. On the other hand, it does seem profitable to begin with the kinds of things that the ordinary layman considers important. Very likely, almost everyone suspects at times that others have treated him in a Machiavellian fashion and is indignant about it. Perhaps most of us, under one stress or another, try our own hand at it from time to time. Certainly, we are all concerned about this phenomenon, and we therefore have reason to be pleased that Guterman has explored this difficult and controversial area of social action and personality.

William J. Goode

Columbia University

Acknowledgments

SPACE DOES not permit acknowledging all of the individuals and groups that have aided me, in one way or another, in the course of this study. I will, therefore, confine these acknowledgments to those whose help has been critical.

The National Institute of Mental Health assisted financially during a large part of the study by awarding me a fellowship (Fellowship Number MPM–15,502) and by partially reimbursing me for research expenses.

The Hotel Corporation of America and the Treadway Inns, in whose hotels the research was carried out, made the valuable time of their personnel available for administration of the questionnaire and subsidized the research by providing free room while I was doing the field work. Yet at no time did either organization attach any conditions to their support or expect anything from me in return. I am deeply grateful for their generosity. I had the cooperation of many individuals in both organizations; here I can mention only the officer of each organization with whom I had my main liaison: Mr. J. M. Judd, of H.C.A., and Mr. Fred J. Eydt, of Treadway Inns.

Carleton University in Ottawa, Canada, underwrote the costs of typing several drafts of the manuscript.

I have had the good fortune to have friends like Stanley K. Henshaw and Robert B. Smith to give me encouragement and to act as a sounding board for my ideas. I am grateful to my wife, Marilyn, for her never ceasing loyalty and patience.

Introduction

TRADITIONALLY THE sociologist's concern with deviant behavior has centered on the more obtrusive type of offense to moral norms—criminality, delinquency, alcoholism, and so forth. This is in part due to the relative ease with which such behavior can be defined and those who have engaged in it identified. Thus governmental statutes define criminal behavior, and arrest or conviction in a court of law serves to identify the subjects to be studied.

More subtle types of unethical behavior cannot be defined so easily. Yet they are just as injurious, if not more so, to the values of a humanistic and democratic society. We have in mind:

The physician who lies to his patient for the latter's "own good," thereby violating his autonomy;

The political leader who distorts the issues and makes irrational appeals to the electorate, thereby making a travesty of reasoned discussion, which is supposed to be an essential of the democratic process;[1]

The university professor who, in his frenzy to build up his prestige and reputation, exploits his students, thereby stifling their independence and creativity;

The businessman who earns a large portion of his income from the tenements of a slum, thereby contributing to the degradation and misery of slum living;

The social scientist who proffers advice on how to manipulate the public, thereby betraying his calling.

Since these individuals have not committed a clear-cut violation of any law, they are more difficult to identify than, say, delinquents and are therefore not as accessible to study. If, however, there is a quality of character

1. A "tough-minded" analyst of democracy such as Joseph Schumpeter might disagree that reasoned discussion is a necessary ingredient of the democratic process. Though such a view may be empirically correct—insofar as it describes what actually goes on in political systems that are regarded as democratic—it by no means provides a normative guide to how politicians in a democratic society ought to act.

which underlies, and is common to, most of these diverse behaviors, we have no need separately to identify and study those who engage in each type of behavior.[2] We can instead center our attention on the underlying character variable. There, indeed, does seem to be such a variable—Machiavellianism.

A further justification of an empirical study of moral character has to do with the distinction between character[3] and behavior. That a person feels little or no attachment to a given set of moral norms does not necessarily mean that, when he is motivated to violate those norms, he will in fact do so. Conversely, individuals with a strong sense of moral "idealism" do not *ipso facto* always refrain from ethically deviant acts. The individual who has no compunctions about cheating will not always cheat. The individual who is deeply committed to honesty may nonetheless cheat on occasion. There is, in short, no one-to-one relationship between character, on the one side, and behavioral conformity to the relevant ethical values, on the other.

The degree to which a relationship does exist is largely conditioned by a number of factors. Among these are the pressures and inducements to violate norms, the climate of opinion toward norm violations prevailing among one's associates, and the presence or absence of effective social control. Our interest here is in the last factor, the effectiveness of social control. By social control is simply meant the punishment of ethical transgressions and the reward of behavior consonant with given moral principles. In general, where effective social control prevails, even people who have a weak level of commitment to normative standards obey them. Where, on the other hand, social control is weak or has broken down, moral character makes much more of a difference. For then perhaps the principal force restraining a person when he is motivated to engage in misdeeds is his character.

This general view of how character and behavior are related receives support from several studies. In one study of lawyers, independent measures of three variables were obtained: (1) an attorney's concern with professional ethics, (2) whether he had committed an ethical violation, and (3) his exposure to effective social control (as indicated by the type of courts and agencies before which he practiced). It was found that when social control was effective, ethical concern affected the rate of violation, but the difference

2. The above catalogue of behaviors is meant to illustrate the more subtle types of ethical problems deserving of social research. We do not mean to imply that a single character variable *necessarily* explains all of these behaviors, although our remarks here are based on the assumption that a variable like Machiavellianism is probably associated with most of them. Whether or not this assumption is justified, is of course an empirical question.

3. We define character here as an inner sense of commitment to a generalized system of normative standards.

in the violation rate between those with high ethical concern and those with low ethical concern was relatively small. The difference was much more marked when social control was weak: then lawyers with low concern were much more likely to violate professional norms than those with high concern.[4]

An experiment utilizing the Machiavellian scale as a measure of character yielded analogous results. The subjects played a three-man, bargaining game in which success depended in part on the value of playing cards in a participant's hand and in part on his cunning and his ability to manipulate his opponents. The game was played under two conditions: in the high visibility condition, all of the the players knew the value of the playing cards in each other's hand; in the low visibility condition, they did not. Under high visibility, the value of a person's hand was the primary determinant of how successful he was. Under low visibility, however, the major determinant of success was the Mach score, the value of the hand making almost no difference in the points scored over a series of games. This was evidently due to the greater effectiveness in manipulating their opponents which low visibility made possible for the Machiavellians.[5]

If, in situations in which social control is ineffective, a person's character has so much influence on the ethicality of his behavior, the next question is: how common are such situations in modern life? One suspects, quite common.

An outstanding example of deficient social control is provided by medical practice. Lacking technical competence in medicine, the patient is unable to ascertain whether his physician is acting in his best interests and is being completely truthful.[6] Nor can the patient turn to another physician for an independent judgment of his doctor's work: the code of ethics of the American Medical Association forbids one physician to express criticism of another physician in the presence of a patient.[7] Added to this is the questionable effectiveness of the profession's grievance machinery.[8] Civil suits in

4. See J. E. Carlin, *Lawyers' Ethics: A Survey of the New York City Bar* (New York: Russell Sage Foundation, 1966), pp. 135–36.

5. See F. Geis, "Machiavellianism and the Manipulation of One's Fellow Man," mimeographed (Report at Annual Meeting of American Psychological Association, September 7, 1964), pp. 11–16.

6. This was demonstrated in a study of 254 hospital patients in the New York City area. See Columbia University School of Public Health and Administrative Medicine, *The Quantity, Quality and Costs of Medical and Hospital Care Secured by a Sample of Teamster Families in the New York Area* (New York, 1962), table 30, p. 79.

7. See *Principles of Medical Ethics of the American Medical Association* (Chicago: American Medical Association, 1953), chap. 6, sec. 4.

8. A Brooklyn internist, for example, who failed to render any assistance to a victim of a gun-shot wound received no more punishment than a month's suspension from the county medical society. See " Doctor Is Censured for Not Giving Aid," *New York Times*, December

the courts, moreover, apparently provide little deterrence to unethical behavior. For one thing, most physicians are unwilling to give expert testimony against a fellow practitioner who is a defendant. Without such testimony, it is difficult for a plaintiff to win a suit even if he has legitimate grounds for going into court.[9] Professional liability insurance, moreover, relieves the doctor of any direct financial loss; such insurance provides not only that the insurance company pay any damages awarded by the court but also that the company be responsible for the legal defense against the suit.[10] Finally, no negative consequences of an extralegal nature (e.g., serious or permanent damage to a physician's practice or reputation) appear to ensue from a suit.[11] Items such as these intimate that medical doctors can engage in unethical behavior with a large measure of impunity.

The same can be said of lawyers, too, judging from an empirical study of the New York City bar. Jerome E. Carlin estimates that "in any given year fewer than 2 per cent of lawyers who violate the generally accepted norms of the bar are formally handled by the official disciplinary machinery; only about 0.02 per cent are publicly sanctioned by being disbarred, suspended, or censured." The deterrent effect of the penalties meted out is probably minimal. For one thing, "the most widespread violations (fraud and solicita-

12, 1964, pp. 1, 21; and "Censured Doctor Keeps Privileges," *New York Times*, December 17, 1964, p. 18.

In January, 1966, the New York State Board of Regents, which is responsible for the licensing of physicians, found two cancer researchers guilty of experimentally injecting live cancer cells into twenty-two patients without their informed consent. The Board of Regents gave no punishment other than a one-year "probation" to the two physicians. See J. Lear, "Do We Need New Rules for Experimenting on People?" *Saturday Review*, February 5, 1966, pp. 61–70.

9. See "Good Samaritans and Liability for Medical Malpractice," *Columbia Law Review*, 64 (1964):1303; and D. S. Rabsamen, "The California Malpractice Picture," *California Medicine*, 99 (1963):293. In reaction to the "conspiracy of silence," the courts of some states have introduced the doctrine of *res ipsa loquitur*, which relieves the plaintiff of the obligation to produce an expert witness in certain kinds of cases.

10. See H. Hassard, "Your Malpractice Insurance Contract," *Journal of the American Medical Association*, 168 (1958):2117–21; and "Coverage and Exclusions of Professional Liability Insurance," *Journal of the American Medical Association*, 170 (1959):813–19. A recent sample survey of 20,000 physicians in the United States disclosed that 94 percent of the respondents had professional liability insurance. See A.M.A. Law Department, "First Results: 1963 Professional Liability Survey," *Journal of the American Medical Association*, 189 (1964):859–66.

11. Evidence for this assertion comes from two empirical studies. See R. L. Wyckoff, "The Effects of a Malpractice Suit Upon Physicians in Connecticut," *Journal of the American Medical Association*, 176 (1961):1101, and "How State Medical Society Executives Size Up Professional Liability," *Journal of the American Medical Association*, 164 (1957):580–82.

tion of clients) generally receive the mildest sanctions and are least likely to be formally adjudicated." In addition, "the record of the proceedings and the charges are not made public" in over half of the disbarments. The author's conclusion is that in New York City, the organized bar "seems to be less concerned with scrutinizing the moral integrity of the profession than with forestalling public criticism and control."[12]

What can be said of the business world? After laboriously documenting the prevalence of criminal behavior in business, E. H. Sutherland argues that corporations are largely able to avoid detection and punishment for their transgressions. There are three factors in this immunity: (1) corporations can select relatively powerless victims (e.g., scattered and unorganized consumers); (2) their crimes are such that proof is difficult (e.g., misrepresentations in advertising); (3) they can use political power and influence to prevent punishment[13]

The foregoing situations appear not to be atypical. In many areas of our society, individuals seem able to engage in unethical behavior and "get away with it." For this reason, moral character is a cardinal determinant of the moral quality of behavior. In addition, the absence of effective social control may itself be due to deficiencies in the modal character patterns of those individuals who occupy positions in a given area. For such absence raises the ominous possibility that the majority of individuals in that area, especially the power holders, do not really want effective control; they themselves may have little commitment to the relevant ethical norms.

In any event, the modal patterns of moral character have a great effect on the moral level of behavior prevalent in a social area. So to study the influences impinging on character is to take one step toward understanding behavior. To be sure, it is only a single step. Other steps are necessary to round out this understanding—studying the forces making for the effectiveness or ineffectiveness of social control, studying variations in modal character patterns, studying the social pattern of inducements to violate norms, etc. Nonetheless, we have to start somewhere.

A principal, although not the exclusive, aim of the present research is to explore the sources of the Machiavellian outlook. In pursuing this aim, the study examines three classic bodies of theory in the social sciences. From these theories we cull empirical propositions, which we then test with the data from a questionnaire survey of hotel employees.

The first chapter is devoted to a description of the Machiavellian index and a discussion of its validity. We also specify the sampling procedures of

12. See Carlin, *Lawyers' Ethics*, pp. 160–62.

13. See E. H. Sutherland, *White Collar Crime* (New York: Dryden Press, 1949), pp. 230–33.

the study and some characteristics of the sample. With these preliminaries out of the way, we go on to scrutinize the Freudian theory of the superego for whatever clues it may provide to the origin of Machiavellianism. Here our interest is in the respondent's recollection of his parents and how they treated him during the period when he was growing up. We also look at the respondent's mode of handling his feelings of aggression. The discussion then turns to the writings of Charles H. Cooley for the suggestions they offer on the role played by " sympathy " and by the need for social approval in the functioning of conscience. Next, we examine the theories of Ferdinand Toennies and Pitirim Sorokin as they bear on the concept of solidarity. Using as indicators the urbanism of the locality the respondent resided in at two stages in his life and the character of his ties to friends and relatives, we explore the relevance of solidarity to Machiavellianism.

Part II of the presentation shifts to an organizational analysis centering on an index of solidary feelings. The data suggest how the morale of personnel in a hotel is influenced by certain properties of the work milieu—specifically, the personality composition of a hotel's employees and the personality characteristics of the management—and by certain predispositions of the individual. We pay particular attention to the interaction of the various factors.

PART I

THE SOURCES OF MACHIAVELLIANISM

CHAPTER 1

Some Notes on Method

The Machiavellian Index

CHARACTERISTICS OF THE INDEX

MACHIAVELLIANISM, as revealed by the content of the scale items designed to measure this variable, refers to an amoral, manipulative attitude toward other individuals, combined with a cynical view of men's motives and of their character. A few of the Machiavellian statements should convey the flavor of the scale.

> Never tell anyone the real reason you did something unless it is useful to do so.
>
> One should take action only when sure that it is morally right.
>
> Generally speaking, men won't work hard unless they are forced to do so.
>
> Most people who get ahead in the world lead clean, moral lives.

The second and fourth statements are "reversed" in the sense that a Machiavellian person is likely to disagree with them.

Developed by Richard Christie, Mach V consists of a series of items in forced-choice format. Social psychologists have devised this format out of a concern with the influence of social desirability—that is, the degree to which it is socially acceptable to attribute a given quality or opinion to oneself—upon responses to attitude and personality items.[1] Many individuals distort their replies to a questionnaire in an attempt to convey a favorable self-image. Formulated with an eye to counteracting this tendency, each item in the forced-choice format consists of a pair of statements. One of the statements is keyed to the variable the scale is supposed to measure. The other refers to a different variable but has been judged by a panel to be equivalent to the first statement in its social desirability. The respondent is

1. For a detailed discussion of social desirability, see A. L. Edwards, *The Social Desirability Variable in Personality Assessment and Research* (New York: Dryden Press, 1957).

asked to indicate which of the two statements he agrees with more or which is more accurately descriptive of his personality.[2]

Here is an example of such an item from the Mach index:

1. It is wise to flatter important people.
2. Once a decision has been made, it is best to keep changing it as new circumstances arise.

The first statement is the Mach statement. If the respondent checks this statement in preference to the second, his response is regarded as a high Mach response. His total scale score is determined by the number of high Mach and low Mach responses to all of the items in the scale.

We have taken twelve forced-choice items from Mach V for use in our index.[3] The index is weighted toward the manipulativeness component since seven of the items tap manipulativeness and only five cynicism. All of the items are listed and the scoring system is described in the Appendix.

Machiavellianism may be viewed from two somewhat different perspectives. Either one can stress the emotional detachment that the Machiavellian exhibits in dealing with others, or one can stress his lack of commitment to conventional moral norms.[4] These two ways of thinking about Mach-

2. Whether the forced-choice technique has, in fact, been entirely successful in cancelling out the effects of social desirability is a controversial question. For data suggesting that it has not, see E. Marks and C. A. Lindsay, "Machiavellian Attitudes: Some Measurement and Behavioral Considerations," *Sociometry*, 29 (1966):228–36. A few of the knotty problems of this technique are intimated in J. E. Milholland, "Theory and Techniques of Assessment," *Annual Review of Psychology*, 15 (1964):314–17. No discussion of these problems will be attempted here since it would take us too far from the main line of our exposition. Suffice it to say that whatever the imperfections of the forced-choice format, it does not, compared to the traditional Likert format, seem to lessen the validity of a measure and probably augments it.

3. In addition to the pair of statements, each item in Mach V has a "buffer" statement which is much lower or much higher in its social desirability value than the pair. The respondent is supposed to rank the three statements. The third statement serves several functions, the main one being further to disguise the nature of the scale. Several considerations have led us to drop it from each of the items in our index. For one thing, the buffer statement would have added considerably to the time it took to administer the questionnaire. In addition, 58 percent of our sample never went beyond high school. We feared that, since our questionnaire was self-administered, many of these people would have found a triad of statements confusing. In view of the considerable amount of assistance we had to give respondents in filling out the questionnaire, this fear appears, in retrospect, to have been justified. To compensate for any loss of disguise which dropping the third statement might have entailed, we interspersed the Mach items in the questionnaire with forced-choice items from other scales.

4. R. Christie distinguishes between these two aspects of the concept in "Some Consequences of Taking Machiavelli Seriously," in E. F. Borgatta and W. W. Lambert, eds., *Handbook of Personality Theory and Research* (Chicago: Rand McNally, 1968), p. 960.

iavellianism are not necessarily in conflict. In fact, they complement each other by drawing attention to different facets of the concept. In the present study, we have chosen to concentrate on the element of amorality. The advantage of this is that it permits us to bring a vast store of theoretical work and empirical studies dealing with the assimilation of ethical norms to bear upon our subject.

VALIDATION STUDIES

Several studies have dealt with the validity of the Mach scale. An early, Likert version of the scale was tested for validity by a rating procedure in which a medical school professor was asked to identify the twenty "most cynical . . . opportunistic" seniors and twenty "most overflowing with love of mankind and human kindness." When the two groups were compared with respect to their scores on the scale, they were found to differ significantly in the expected direction.[5]

If the scale is valid, high scorers should display greater tendencies toward manipulative behavior than low scorers, all other things being equal. Validity in this sense has been cogently demonstrated in an experiment in which each of the subjects—twenty-seven male college students—was assigned the task of administering a personality test to "other subjects" who, in actuality, were stooges of the experimenter. The "testers" were given explicit instructions to manipulate, "to use your power arbitrarily—to confuse or distract the subject [i.e., stooge] who will be taking the test." Under the prompting of these instructions, the Machiavellians engaged in a significantly greater number of manipulative acts than the non-Machiavellians. Moreover, they used a greater variety of ploys and were more inclined to say that they enjoyed the experience.[6]

In a second experiment, the subjects played a three-person game in which each player moved a marker along the path of a game board. Winning consisted of reaching the end of the path ahead of other players. The number of spaces advanced at a given turn depended jointly on the value of the dice thrown and on the value of the "power cards" in a player's hand. In order to be successful over a series of games, a subject had to be able to manipulate the other players by inducing an opponent to join a coalition even though it might not be in his interest to do so and by taking advantage, in various ways, of the partner once a coalition had been formed. The Machiavellians

5. See R. Christie and R. K. Merton, "Procedures for the Sociological Study of the Value Climate of Medical Schools," *Journal of Medical Education*, 33 (1958):136.

6. This experiment is described in detail in F. Geis, "Machiavellianism and the Manipulation of One's Fellow Man," mimeographed (Report at Annual Meeting of American Psychological Association, September 7, 1964), pp. 3–10.

were far more successful in playing this game than their less Machiavellian opponents.[7]

The foregoing studies seem to substantiate the validity of the Mach scale as a measure of a cynical, amoral outlook and of the tendency and ability to manipulate others.

Field Work Procedures

Our interest in the hotel industry as a setting for the research initially developed in response to an article by one of the leading executives of the Hotel Corporation of America.[8] Dealing with the ethical conflicts faced by the modern businessman, the article concluded with a plea for research on morality in business. When we approached H.C.A. requesting access to its personnel for purposes of the study, the corporation readily consented.

Most of the H.C.A. units, as we soon found out, were located in large cities and suburbs. This was felt to be a serious drawback for the research since the size of the community the respondent worked and lived in would probably be an important variable. Consequently, it seemed desirable to add hotels located in small-town settings to the sample. With this consideration in mind, we communicated with several other chains, and one of these, Treadway Inns, proved to be agreeable to the study.

In deciding which hotels in the two chains would be included in the investigation, we made no attempt to secure a random sample. Hotels, rather, were selected with a view to minimizing the amount of travel that would have to be done in the course of the field work. Limitations in the research budget necessitated this departure from ideal sampling procedures.

The sample consisted of 483 employees in twenty-six hotels located in the eastern coastal states between Washington, D.C., and Bangor, Maine. All of the hotels were year-round establishments for transients. Because giving a self-administered questionnaire to manual workers would have created insurmountable problems, the sample was confined to employees on the white-collar and managerial levels. Among the types of personnel included were general managers and their assistants, heads of various departments, front office clerks, switchboard operators, headwaiters, chefs, accountants, bookkeepers, security officers, and secretaries. In twenty-three of the hotels, the sample was simply defined as all white-collar and managerial employees. In the three largest hotels, there were too many such employees to include all in the sample, so we stratified the population by the respondent's type of

7. See ibid., pp. 11–16.

8. See R. P. Sonnabend, "The Ethical Dilemmas of Businessmen," *Challenge*, January 1962, pp. 28–30.

work, set a sample quota for each type, and selected a random sample from each stratum.

The field work was conducted in the autumn of 1963 and the winter of 1964. Each respondent filled out a highly structured, self-administered questionnaire, which took on the average an hour and a half to complete. Usually the hotel management set aside a room in which groups of respondents assembled to take the questionnaire on company time. The number of respondents filling out the questionnaire at the same sitting varied from one to ten or fifteen. As each respondent finished the questionnaire, we briefly checked it over and had him correct any gross errors.

To maximize the candor of replies to the questionnaire, it was important to convince respondents that no information about individuals would be disclosed to the management. In addition to oral and written assurances of confidentiality and to not requiring the respondent to identify himself in the questionnaire, we took several steps to demonstrate our good faith. Accompanying each questionnaire was a letter on university stationery emphasizing the purely academic nature of the research and promising to send each respondent a summary of the preliminary findings. This promise was later kept. On the first page of the instrument, moreover, was an "official acknowledgment" of financial assistance from the United States Department of Health, Education, and Welfare.

Finally, participation in the study was voluntary. Respondents were expressly told that they could refuse to fill out a questionnaire if they so wished. We permitted nonparticipation with full consciousness that it might vitiate the representativeness of the sample. Aside from our belief that social scientists have no right morally to force people to participate in their research and aside from our probable inability in most instances to make individuals participate, there was a pragmatic reason for this practice. Had we been seeking information about individuals in order to turn over such information to management, most respondents would have expected us to permit no refusals. The policy of keeping participation voluntary was thus designed to underscore our independence of management.

There were three hotels in which the refusal rate exceeded 30 percent. In one of them, the person in charge of personnel records informed the other employees that we were collecting the addresses of all respondents (a step taken in order to ascertain the census tract in which each respondent lived). This leak evidently created considerable suspicion toward the study. The two other hotels had been the scene of the preliminary field work and the pretesting. The personal character of many of the items asked in the pretest apparently made many persons reluctant to participate. Sufficient time elapsed between the pretest and the administration of the questionnaire for this opposition to crystallize.

In one of these latter hotels, an additional factor was at work. The chain was about to relinquish operation of the hotel. A widespread knowledge of this fact led to considerable bitterness among personnel toward the chain, divided the management into factions, and weakened managerial authority. Employees were aware that our access to the hotel was obtained through the chain, and they apparently identified the research with the chain. The result was that many employees felt little inclination to cooperate.

The three hotels with exceptionally high refusal rates were offset by fourteen hotels in which virtually everyone selected for the sample cooperated.

Characteristics of the Sample

The hotels varied widely in size, as indicated by the number of employees. Approximately half of the respondents came from three giant urban hotels, each of which had no less than 700 personnel. At the other extreme, about 30 percent of the sample worked for units having less than 90 employees each.

The hotels were located by and large in three urban areas—New York, Boston, and Washington, D.C. About three-quarters of the respondents worked for hotels situated in these cities or their suburbs. But a fairly sizable number—25 percent of the sample—were employed in small towns, the overwhelming majority of these in communities with a population of under 25,000.

Almost two-thirds of the sample consisted of males. There was a fairly even distribution of respondents on the age variable, those in the "50 and over" age category, however, being somewhat more numerous than those in the other three age categories (18–29, 30–39, and 40–49).

A Note on Tests of Significance

Because our sample is not a probability sample, tests of significance of the statistical associations presented in this study are, strictly speaking, not appropriate. Such tests, moreover, have been the object of debate in the last fifteen years. Some authors argue that they are not applicable to research whose chief purpose is the exploring and uncovering of causal relationships.[9] We happen to believe that those who are opposed to the tests have the better

9. The most lucid statement of the antitest position that we are aware of is contained in S. M. Lipset, M. A. Trow, and J. S. Coleman, *Union Democracy* (Glencoe: The Free Press, 1956), Appendix I, pp. 427–32. A recent discussion of the debate on tests, with a good bibliography, is D. E. Morrison and R. E. Henkel, "Significance Tests Reconsidered," *American Sociologist*, 4 (1969):131–40.

of the argument. Nevertheless many, perhaps most, social scientists continue to give credence to the tests. This, of course, poses a dilemma. Should we omit the tests? To do so would satisfy our own conscience, but would leave many readers dissatisfied. In the face of this dilemma, we have settled for a compromise—namely, to register our disbelief in the tests but nonetheless to attach significance levels to our tables for the benefit of those readers who place reliance on the orthodox procedures.

We have employed the chi-square test throughout. In all tables, the test data are given immediately beneath the cross-tabulation. In three-variable tables, the presentation of the test results is somewhat complex. We have computed a separate chi-square for each row and each column. Each cell in such tables is denoted by a letter. In a four-cell table, for instance, the cells are lettered as in figure 1. In presenting the chi-square data, we have

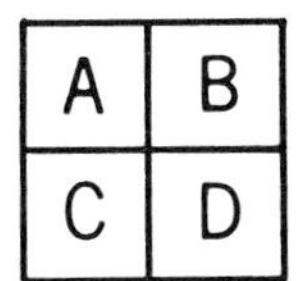

FIGURE 1

prefixed the test results for the first row by A vs. B; those for the first column by A vs. C; and so forth. The cells of a three-variable table with six cells are denoted as illustrated in figure 2. The chi-square test for the first row is designated by A vs. B vs. C; the test for the first column by A

A	B	C
D	E	F

FIGURE 2

vs. D. To get a clearer idea of our procedures, the reader might wish to examine the chi-square results for the three-variable table on page 26 before he proceeds.

In two-variable tables, columns occasionally total 99 or 101 percent due to rounding of percentages.

CHAPTER 2

The Family Milieu during the Early Years

The Freudian Theory of the Superego

THE FIRST THEORY we shall examine in seeking to illuminate the sources of Machiavellianism is Freud's theory of the superego—that entity in the personality which he conceives of as embodying each individual's moral code.[1] This theory is largely devoted to two separate but interrelated questions. The first concerns the origins of the superego: how does the superego arise; what are the circumstances and processes initially accounting for its formation? The second has to do with the severity of conscience: what accounts for variations in severity; why is it that the superegos of some individuals are harsh, embracing strict standards, while those of other persons are lenient, inclined toward permissive values?

THE ORIGIN OF THE SUPEREGO

The point of departure for Freud's answer to the first of these questions is his concept of identification. Freud distinguishes between two ways in which a child can relate to a parent (as well as to other persons). On the one hand, a child may choose a parent as an object of cathexis: he may have a sexual desire for the parent. On the other hand, a child may identify with a parent: he may seek to imitate the parent, to model one or more aspects of his own behavior on that of the parent.[2]

The little boy develops, in the earliest years, an object cathexis for the mother and an identification with the father. For a while, these tendencies

1. The following are the principal writings of Freud on the superego: S. Freud, "On Narcissism—An Introduction," in J. Strachey, trans. and ed., *The Standard Edition of the Complete Psychological Works of Sigmund Freud* (London: Hogarth Press, 1957), vol. 14; S. Freud, *The Ego and the Id*, trans. and ed. J. Strachey, *The Standard Edition of the Complete Psychological Works of Sigmund Freud* (London: Hogarth Press, 1961), vol. 19; S. Freud, *Civilization and Its Discontents* (New York: W. W. Norton and Company, 1962); and S. Freud, *New Introductory Lectures on Psychoanalysis* (New York: W. W. Norton and Company, 1933).

2. See Freud, *New Introductory Lectures on Psychoanalysis*, pp. 90–91. An elaborate account of identification is to be found in S. Freud, *Group Psychology and the Analysis of the Ego*, trans. and ed. J. Strachey, *The Standard Edition of the Complete Psychological Works of Sigmund Freud* (London: Hogarth Press, 1955), vol. 18, chap. 7.

coexist without any conflict. Then, as the sexual craving for the mother becomes more intense, the attitude toward the father becomes ambivalent; the boy becomes hostile toward the father since the latter has sexual rights with the mother. This situation brings the child into increasing conflict with the parents and produces in the son a dread of his father, who, he fears, will in the heat of jealousy castrate him. The object cathexis for the mother, combined with a hostile, jealous attitude toward the father, is what Freud calls the Oedipus complex. In order to end this tense situation, the boy gives up the incestuous craving for his mother and represses the hostile side of the ambivalence he feels toward the father. As the object cathexis is renounced, the energy used in the cathexis will be diverted either to an intensification of his identification with the father or to the development of an identification with the mother.

Which of these courses the boy's psychological development takes, depends, according to Freudian theory, on the relative prominence of the masculine and feminine components in his constitutional make-up. Ordinarily the masculine elements are sufficiently strong for an intensification of his relation with his father to occur. Sometimes, though, the feminine components of his constitution are prominent and the identification is with his mother.[3]

The emotional life of the little girl progresses along somewhat different lines. According to Freud, it is the father, not the mother, toward whom she directs her cathexis. As a result of this cathexis, she becomes jealous of her mother. Since the daughter has no penis, nothing like the fear of castration can operate to bring about the dissolution of the Oedipus complex. Consequently the girl's complex continues indefinitely and is abandoned only "late in life and then incompletely." Nonetheless identifications eventually do replace her object cathexis for the father.[4]

Freud's ideas concerning the history of the child's emotional life have been somewhat oversimplified in the above paragraphs. In addition to erotic love toward the parent of the opposite sex and ambivalence toward the parent of the same sex, the Oedipus complex includes subsidiary tendencies just the opposite of these but existing simultaneously with them. Each child develops an object cathexis for the parent of the same sex; the boy comes to have an erotic love for his father, the girl for her mother. Accompanying these cathexes are ambivalent feelings toward the other parent. Thus an inverted Oedipus complex coexists with the positive complex. The relative weight of the two complexes in a child's psychological functioning varies

3. See Freud, *The Ego and the Id*, pp. 32–34, and Freud, *New Introductory Lectures on Psychoanalysis*, pp. 91–92.

4. See Freud, *New Introductory Lectures on Psychoanalysis*, lecture 33.

from individual to individual. Some children have only a positive complex, some only an inverted complex, while others have both complexes, one or the other being dominant.

Upon the resolution or weakening of the Oedipus complex, the identifications which emerge will be based, according to Freud, not only on the positive complex but on the inverted complex as well. Thus, if a child has both complexes, he may develop identifications with both parents.

In developing the postoedipal identifications, the little boy or the little girl adopts the moral prohibitions and ideals of the parent (or parents). As Freud expresses it: "The broad outcome" of these processes is "the forming of a precipitate in the ego consisting of those two identifications [that with the father and that with the mother] in some way united with each other." It is this precipitate that constitutes the superego of Freudian theory.[5]

GUILT AND THE SEVERITY OF THE SUPEREGO

The second major problem to which Freud addresses himself in the theory of the superego is the severity of the conscience. Why do individuals react with guilt when violating an ethical norm? Why do some feel guilty even when they have, in fact, committed no violation but have simply, in a moment of temptation, contemplated doing so?

Freud's answers to these questions are connected with his notions of how the personality handles aggression. He postulates two basic classes of instincts. One of these, Eros, or the life instincts, corresponds to the bodily needs of self-preservation and procreation. By "bringing about a more and more far-reaching combination of the particles into which living substance is dispersed, 'Eros' aims at complicating life and at the same time, of course, at preserving it." The death instincts, by contrast, seek "to lead organic life back into the inanimate state." An important constituent of the death instincts is aggression. Here, as with the other instincts, Freud postulates a quantum of energy which can be displaced from one object to another. If aggression is prevented from being channeled toward one object, it will seek out another object. A severe conscience, according to Freud, results from the aggressive instincts of a person being directed against his own ego. Guilt is aggression turned inward.[6]

Freud's views on how this turning inward is achieved changed over the years. In his first writings on superego functioning, *The Ego and the Id*, the explanation is "instinctual defusion." One of Freud's basic notions is that different instincts may be blended—or as he phrases it, "fused"—with

5. See Freud, *The Ego and the Id*, pp. 31–34.
6. See ibid., pp. 40–47.

each other as they are manifested in behavior. For instance, the child's object cathexis for the parent of the opposite sex in the Oedipus complex has "a sadistic component." It partakes not only of the life instincts but of the death instincts as well. If fusion of the different instincts is possible, so is defusion. Instincts which have hitherto been manifested in combination at the behavioral level may separate and come to operate independently of each other. This is particularly likely to happen when an object cathexis can no longer be discharged and the component instincts must find new outlets.[7]

In Freud's initial ideas about superego formation, such a defusion occurs with the dissolution of the Oedipus complex. The oedipal object cathexis of the child for one of his parents combines sexual elements with aggressiveness. The identification which follows the abandoning of the Oedipus complex involves a sublimation of the erotic component. The energy that previously underlay the erotic love for a parent is now used in the child's personality for internalizing the prohibitions and ideals of parental authority. When this happens, however, the aggressive element in the object cathexis must find a new outlet since, for reasons which Freud leaves unspecified, it cannot be used in identifying with the parents. This aggressiveness comes to be directed against the ego and to constitute the motive power in the functioning of conscience. Defusion, then, is "the source of the general character of harshness and cruelty exhibited by the ideal [i.e., the superego]—its dictatorial 'Thou shalt'."[8]

This first formulation of Freud's concerning the origin of the superego's guilt feelings is strictly on an intrapsychic level. "Object cathexis," "identification," "aggressive instincts," "defusion"—these all refer to what is happening in the child's mind and, therefore, do not permit us to derive hypotheses relating aspects of the superego to occurrences in the child's environment. The revised formulation offered in *Civilization and Its Discontents* remedies this shortcoming.

In this latter formulation, the principal motive associated with the development of conscience is the dread of losing parental love. The parents lay down the standards which determine what is to be called good and what is to be called bad. In making the child conform to their standards, they cause him to renounce much instinctual gratification. Initially, these renunciations are made out of the fear of parental authority. The child naturally reacts to the frustration of his impulses by an unleashing of aggressiveness. But this aggressiveness cannot be exhibited openly, lest the parents' love—which the child, as a powerless and dependent creature, needs for its existence—be forfeited. Therefore, the child turns his rage and

7. See ibid., p. 41.
8. Ibid., p. 54.

aggressiveness inward: they are taken over by the superego and directed toward the ego, becoming manifest as guilt feelings. Each time the child is forced to renounce gratification of some instinctual impulse either by the parents or by his superego, there is a repetition of this process and the superego is strengthened—that is to say, the amount of guilt felt by the child increases.

If, then, a strict conscience stems from inwardly directed aggression, the level of this aggression, in turn, seems to be largely a function of two variables. The first of these is the strictness of the child's upbringing—that is, the amount of instinctual gratification the parents require the child to give up. The more such renunciations the child is compelled to make, the more hostility he feels. The second variable is the amount of love the parents have for the child. Where this love is absent or is defective, the child's motive for not directing its hostility at the parents is weakened and consequently a strong sense of guilt does not develop.[9]

The later version of Freud's ideas about the sources of guilt feelings thus has a theoretical advantage over the earlier version inasmuch as it links intrapsychic processes, such as the displacement of aggression, to extrapsychic events. In doing so, it tells us something about how the development of guilt is affected by parental treatment of a child.

The Empirical Findings

Whatever the shortcomings of Freud's theory, it has nonetheless proved of immense value in generating hypotheses for research on moral attitudes and behavior. In the following sections, we shall examine previous studies that bear on some of these hypotheses, and we shall also present relevant data from the present research. No systematic attempt has been made to glean every hypothesis which could conceivably be found in the theory of the superego. Some phases of the theory appear too complicated or too indefinite to lend themselves to statement in the form of hypotheses. (Freud's discussion of the several possible forms that the Oedipus complex can take, is a case in point.) The exposition here, moreover, will deal only with those hypotheses which are subject to testing with the data from our own study.

Several qualifications are necessary before turning to a discussion of the empirical findings. According to Freud, the process of superego formation begins with the dissolution of the Oedipus complex at about the age of five. He never clearly tells us, however, when the process ends, so that the time span required for the formation of conscience is left obscure.[10] Presumably

9. See Freud, *Civilization and Its Discontents*, chap. 7.

10. Freud's ambiguity on this point shows up, for example, when we compare *The Ego and the Id*, p. 37, with *New Introductory Lectures on Psychoanalysis*, p. 92.

a large part of the process takes place prior to puberty. But many of the studies cited below are based on measures referring to events during adolescence. Though the empirical research is, in general, consistent with Freudian theory inasmuch as it deals with variables generated by the theory, this research nevertheless fails—insofar as it focuses on the period of the teens—to provide a strict test of the theory.

Most of the investigations, moreover, deal with consciously held moral values or with behavior whose moral significance a person can recognize. But Freud's concept of the superego embraces unconscious elements, which, he thinks, play an important role in the psychic functioning. For this reason, the extent to which the moral variables in the empirical investigations correspond to the concept of the superego is problematic. Although there is overlap, it is doubtful that any single variable can capture the rich complexity of the Freudian concept.

PARENTAL STANDARDS

Central to Freud's theory of superego formation is the concept of identification. The child acquires his own standards and values by taking over those of his parents. This process, however, reveals nothing about the nature of the standards internalized. The child, according to Freud, internalizes parental standards whether these accord with the morality generally prevailing in the society or not. If the moral attitudes of the parents are deviant, the child, one can infer, will develop a conscience whose contents are deviant. These considerations imply that one determinant of the child's moral outlook is the moral outlook of his parents. Several empirical studies corroborate this view.[11]

H. Hartshorne and M. A. May found that cheating among children was associated with antisocial or deviant behavior in parents.[12] Another part of their inquiries examined children's ideas of right and wrong as related to the ideas held by other groups in the environment. The highest association, as revealed by a correlation of .55, was that for the parents. This suggests

11. In fairness to the reader, we should note that the measurement of parental conscience in these investigations is not entirely satisfactory from our standpoint. Freud makes a strict distinction between the parents' moral behavior and their superegos, pointing out that the two do not necessarily coincide. It is the parents' superegos, Freud argues, not the standards implicit in their behavior, which the child internalizes. Several studies, however, measure parental morality by behavioral indicators, such as a criminal record. Despite this inadequacy, these studies illuminate the influence of parental attitudes on children's morality and therefore warrant discussion. See Freud, *New Introductory Lectures on Psychoanalysis*, p. 95.

12. See H. Hartshorne and M. A. May, *Studies in the Nature of Character: I Studies in Deceit* (New York: Macmillan, 1930), pp. 284, 294.

that the ethical attitudes of parents exert a stronger influence on children than those of other groups.

A second study containing evidence about the ethical standards of parents, Sheldon and Eleanor Glueck's inquiry into juvenile delinquency, measured such standards by "the presence of immorality, drunkenness, and criminality" in the home.[13] Unfortunately their measure referred not only to the behavior of the child's parents but to that of his siblings as well. Nevertheless, the data are relevant insofar as they showed that deviant conduct was present in a higher proportion of the delinquents' homes than of the non-delinquents' homes.[14]

In the present investigation, we have attempted to tap the respondent's recollection of the moral values of his parents by an index of the perceived Machiavellianism of the parents. This index utilizes two types of items.

TABLE 2.1
PERCENT HIGH ON MACHIAVELLIANISM BY PERCEIVED MACHIAVELLIANISM OF PARENTS

	Father's Perceived Mach		
	Low	*Medium*	*High*
% High Mach	23% (156)	31% (119)	39% (148)
	$\chi^2 = 9.220$; df = 2; .01 > p > .005.		
	Mother's Perceived Mach		
	Low	*Medium*	*High*
% High Mach	26% (173)	30% (123)	40% (158)
	$\chi^2 = 7.563$; df = 2; .025 > p > .01.		
	Same-Sex Parent's Perceived Mach		
	Low	*Medium*	*High*
% High Mach	18% (96)	32% (177)	40% (157)
	$\chi^2 = 13.805$; df = 2; p < .005.		

13. See S. Glueck and E. Glueck, *Unraveling Juvenile Delinquency* (Cambridge, Mass.: Harvard University Press for the Commonwealth Fund, 1950), p. 111.

14. The manner in which the standards and evaluations of adult authorities influence children is illuminated in an ingenious experiment of Bandura and McDonald. See A. Bandura and F. J. McDonald, "The Influence of Social Reinforcement and the Behavior of Models in Shaping Children's Moral Judgments," *Journal of Abnormal and Social Psychology*, 67 (1963):274–82.

One gives a statement from the Machiavellian scale and asks the respondent to indicate the extent to which each of his parents would, in the respondent's judgment, agree or disagree with the statement. The second kind, in effect, asks the respondent to make global judgments of how Machiavellian his parents were. Each kind is represented by two items—one designed to get at cynicism, the other at manipulativeness.

Table 2.1 indicates a fairly sizable correlation between the perceived Machiavellianism of the parents and the respondent's score on the Mach scale. Assuming that the perceived Mach variable measures—if perhaps crudely—actual differences in the Machiavellianism of a respondent's parents, the data suggest that one source of a person's Machiavellianism is the attitudes held by his parents during the period when he is being socialized.

PARENTAL LOVE

The dread of losing the parents' love is a cardinal element in Freud's theory of superego development. It is the child's original motive for obeying his parents. It affects, moreover, the way in which the child handles the aggressiveness released by the forced renunciation of his instinctual impulses. Fearful of losing parental love if he directs his hostility against them, he turns it inward against his own ego and transforms it into feelings of guilt, which provide the motive power for the superego. A corollary is that the extent to which the child internalizes ethical norms varies with the amount of love he receives from his parents. If his parents do not show him much affection, he has little to lose by disobeying them or by directing aggression against them.

R. F. Peck's and R. J. Havighurst's intensive longitudinal research on thirty-four adolescents in a small midwestern town supports the above corollary.[15] This study reported that "mutual trust and approval among family members"—a factor analytic variable which roughly corresponds to the degree of love the parents showed the child—highly correlated with the strength of the child's conscience. In an investigation of male college freshmen,[16] the degree to which respondents perceived their parents as "emotionally supportive and warm" was negatively associated with scores on the psychopathic deviate scale of the MMPI.[17]

15. See R. F. Peck and R. J. Havighurst, *The Psychology of Character Development* (New York: John Wiley, 1960), pp. 103–8, 255–58.

16. See P. E. Slater, "Psychological Factors in Role Specialization" (Ph.D. diss., Harvard University, 1955).

17. For a discussion of the validity of the psychopathic deviate scale, see L. J. Cronbach, *Essentials of Psychological Testing*, 2d ed. (New York: Harper and Brothers, 1960), pp. 492–95.

The relation of parental love to the internalization of ethical norms has also been evidenced at younger age levels. In their study of 379 five-year-olds, R. R. Sears, E. Maccoby, and H. Levin found that the level of conscience was related to several aspects of maternal behavior reflecting the amount of affection given the child.[12] For one thing, evidence of maternal rejection of the child correlated negatively with the development of conscience when the amount of dependency exhibited by the child and the sex of the child were held constant. Furthermore, maternal "warmth" toward the child was found to be positively associated with the development of conscience. These two variables, however, exhibited a strong correlation only if the mother used "withdrawal of love" fairly often for disciplinary purposes. This type of discipline included such techniques as the expression of hurt or disappointment at the child's misdeeds.[19]

This finding fits in neatly with Freud's ideas in that it suggests that not only is a high degree of affection necessary for the child to fear the loss of parental love, but also the parents must occasionally withdraw their love for this fear to take hold. Otherwise, the child will come to believe that, regardless of how he behaves, he need have no fear of losing the parents' affection.[20]

In the present research, the measurement of the parental dimension is based on items referring to the degree of "closeness" or "rapport" that the respondent recalls as having existed between himself and his parents during his teens. The rapport index consists of three items, one inquiring about the frequency with which each parent participated in leisure-time activities with the respondent, a second about the extent to which each parent was effective in helping his children with the emotional crises of adolescence, and a third about the frequency with which the respondent confided in each parent.

18. See R. R. Sears, E. Maccoby, and H. Levin, *Patterns of Child Rearing* (Evanston, Ill.: Row, Peterson, and Company, 1957), pp. 382–84 and 387–89.

19. Using the same measure of conscience, Burton and his associates replicated these findings in a study of seventy-seven nursery-school pupils. See R. V. Burton et al., "Antecedents of Resistance to Temptation in Four-Year-Old Children," *Child Development*, 32 (1961): 689–710.

20. Evidence for the role of parental affection in the child's moral development is also to be found in studies of juvenile delinquency. See A. Bandura and R. H. Walters, *Adolescent Aggression: A Study of the Influence of Child-Training Practices and Family Interrelationships* (New York: Ronald Press, 1959), pp. 48–54, 80–83; and S. Glueck and E. Glueck, *Unraveling Juvenile Delinquency*, pp. 125–30. These studies are relevant here inasmuch as the authors of both books argue that the failure to internalize socially acceptable ethical norms is a distinguishing characteristic of delinquents, and Bandura and Walters present evidence substantiating these arguments. See Bandura and Walters, *Adolescent Aggression*, pp. 254, 287–90, 302–8; and Glueck and Glueck, *Unraveling Juvenile Delinquency*, pp. 181–82.

Although the third item does not directly ask about the parents' attitudes or behavior toward the respondent, it was included on the assumption that a person would not be likely to have confided in a parent who rejected him or was hostile toward him.

Table 2.2 presents the cross-tabulation between Machiavellianism and perceived rapport with each of the parents and the cross-tabulation between Machiavellianism and perceived rapport with the parent of the same sex as the respondent. In each case, the higher the perceived rapport, the less likely is a respondent to be Machiavellian.

TABLE 2.2
PERCENT HIGH ON MACHIAVELLIANISM BY PERCEIVED RAPPORT WITH PARENTS

	Rapport with Father		
	Low	*Medium*	*High*
% High Mach	41% (194)	23% (120)	22% (104)
	$\chi^2 = 16.519$; df = 2; $p < .005$.		
	Rapport with Mother		
	Low	*Medium*	*High*
% High Mach	38% (213)	28% (152)	22% (93)
	$\chi^2 = 9.247$; df = 2; $.01 > p > .005$.		
	Rapport with Same-Sex Parent		
	Low	*Medium*	*High*
% High Mach	43% (108)	31% (187)	23% (136)
	$\chi^2 = 10.983$; df = 2; $p < .005$.		

PUNITIVENESS OF THE PARENTS

One factor in superego development that Freud mentions from time to time but does not deal with as systematically as some of the other factors is the "severity of upbringing." He assumes that the strictness of conscience reflects how severely the parents treat the child. *Severity*, however, is an ambiguous term in Freud's writings. It appears in some passages to connote the extent to which parents employ harsh methods—such as physical punishment, deprivation of privileges, threats of punishment, and verbal assault—in securing compliance from their children. Judging from other passages, however, it could also be interpreted to mean the firmness with ı the parents uphold certain standards to which the child is expected to ırm.[21] Although these two elements of parental behavior may be correlated, they are nevertheless conceptually distinct. In order to keep the two separate in our minds, the first will be termed punitiveness and the second strictness.

Punitiveness has received a considerable amount of attention in empirical research, but the findings are generally contrary to what one would expect on the basis of Freud's writings. One of the earliest studies in this area was D. W. MacKinnon's experiment on cheating among college students in a problem-solving situation.[22] Basing his measures on the recollections of the subjects, he found that a higher proportion of the fathers of the noncheaters than those of the cheaters had used "psychological" disciplinary procedures. Their method of discipline had been to make the child feel that he had fallen short of some ideal or that he had hurt his parents and, therefore, that he was less loved by them. In contrast, the fathers of the cheaters had, to a greater extent, used physical punishment, thereby encouraging anger, stubbornness, and resentment on the part of the children.

These findings have been corroborated in research on children. In their study of kindergarten pupils, Sears and his associates found that youngsters of the mothers who used praise and reasoning in inculcating proper standards of behavior tended to have more developed consciences than those whose mothers did not employ these techniques.[23] Parental withdrawal of love also correlated with a high development of conscience, but only where the maternal relation to the child was a warm, affectionate one. Thus the use of lenient, mild procedures in inculcating standards of behavior seem to have favored the internalization of standards. The opposite effects of harsh treatment are suggested in several other findings of this study. These were that mothers who resorted to physical punishment and deprivation of privileges (e.g., forbidding the child to go to the movies) were more likely to have children with defective consciences than mothers who did not make use of these procedures.[24]

21. Freud's equivocal use of the term is seen by comparing *Civilization and Its Discontents*, pp. 76, 84–85, where it seems to signify punitiveness, with *New Introductory Lectures on Psychoanalysis*, p. 75, where it connotes parental firmness.

22. See D. W. MacKinnon, "Violation of Prohibitions," in H. A. Murray, *Explorations in Personality* (New York: Oxford University Press, 1938), pp. 491–501.

23. See Sears, Maccoby, and Levin, *Patterns of Child Rearing*, pp. 387–89.

24. Employing the same operational definition of conscience, Burton and his colleagues came up with remarkably similar findings in a sample of four-year-olds. See Burton et al., "Antecedents of Resistance." Also see M. L. Hoffman, "The Role of the Parent in the Child's Moral Growth," *Religious Education*, 57 (1962): Research Supplement, 18–33; Glueck and Glueck, *Unraveling Juvenile Delinquency*, pp. 132–33; and Bandura and Walters, *Adolescent Aggression*, p. 241, for further data corroborating the findings discussed here.

The index of punitiveness used in the present study consists of two items. One inquires about the respondent's recollections of the frequency with which each parent administered corporal punishment to the respondent as a child. The second tries to get at the perceived degree to which the father and the mother sought to avoid punishment in socializing their children: it asks about the extent to which each parent "tried to reason with his (her) children when they misbehaved, rather than using some form of punishment."

Cross-tabulating Machiavellianism with the three indices of parental punitiveness yields substantial correlations (table 2.3). The more a respondent perceives his parents as having been punitive, the more likely he is to be a Machiavellian.

TABLE 2.3
PERCENT HIGH ON MACHIAVELLIANISM BY THE PERCEIVED PUNITIVENESS OF THE PARENTS

	Father's Punitiveness		
	Low	*Medium*	*High*
% High Mach	21% (152)	33% (154)	41% (116)
	$\chi^2 = 13.186$; df = 2; $p < .005$.		
	Mother's Punitiveness		
	Low	*Medium*	*High*
% High Mach	22% (85)	30% (256)	41% (118)
	$\chi^2 = 8.157$; df = 2; $.025 > p > .01$.		
	Punitiveness, Same-Sex Parent		
	Low	*Medium*	*High*
% High Mach	21% (141)	32% (170)	42% (123)
	$\chi^2 = 13.488$; df = 2; $p < .005$.		

The preponderance of the evidence suggests that, if Freud meant by severity of training the degree of punitiveness parents exhibit in disciplining their children, he was mistaken in believing that severity favors greater internalization of ethical standards. The contrary seems to be true: harsh, fear-provoking treatment on the part of parents is associated with a defective development of conscience. The more "psychological" or "love-oriented" methods of securing compliance with parental standards and restrictions appear, on the other hand, to encourage a greater development of internalized controls.[25]

How this pattern of findings is to be accounted for is not entirely clear. J. W. M. Whiting and I. L. Child offer one possible explanation. They believe that disciplinary techniques vary in the extent to which they keep "the child oriented toward the goal of parental affections." Some punishments hinder the development of a craving for parental love. The punitive

25. Not all of the evidence with respect to punitiveness is consistent. One of the factors used by Peck and Havighurst in their study of adolescents was entitled "Severity of Parental Control." (See Peck and Havighurst, *Psychology of Character Development*, pp. 103–8, 255–58.) It was found to have a positive correlation with two of their variables measuring conscience and a negative correlation with only one of the moral variables—and the latter correlation was very slight. This discrepancy, however, becomes understandable when we examine the character of the severity factor. According to the authors, it had two components. One had to do with the extent to which physical and/or mental punishment was employed by the parent. Hence this component appears to have matched the concept of punitiveness. But the second component was conceptually different, for it referred to the amount of parental control over the child and appears to have been more akin to the concept of strictness than to that of punitiveness. We suspect that the anomalous results of this study were due to the confounding of elements which, in our view, are conceptually distinct.

Three studies that focus on resistance to temptation failed to find a positive relationship between "psychological" discipline and conformity to norms. (An exception to this pattern is that in one of the studies parental withdrawal of love was associated with resistance to deviation.) The dependent variable in each of these investigations was based on whether or not the subject violated the rules of the game he played in an experimental test situation. Two of these studies dealt with children of preschool age. (See Burton et al., "Antecedents of Resistance" and R. R. Sears et al., *Identification and Child Rearing* [London: Tavistock Publications, 1966], pp. 228–32.) If we assume that the effects of psychological discipline upon moral behavior is mediated by the extent to which a person builds up internalized controls, the absence of positive correlations in these studies is perfectly comprehensible. The subjects were too young to have developed internalized standards strong enough to control their behavior. Hence variables that operated by affecting internalization could not show their full effects.

The subjects in the third study were eleven- and twelve-year-old children. (See R. E. Grinder, "Parental Childrearing Practices, Conscience, and Resistance to Temptation of Sixth Grade Children," *Child Development*, 33 [1962]: 803–20.) Therefore, the above arguments would not be applicable. We are not certain just what the explanation for the discrepant findings are in this case. One possibility, however, is raised by Hoffman, who points out that measures of moral behavior that are based on performance in a test situation are subject to extraneous influences. Studies using such measures have heretofore failed to control for the motivation to do well in the game or on the test. "Not cheating for some . . . may then signify disinterest in the prize or perhaps low achievement strivings in general rather than a strong conscience." (Hoffman, "The Role of the Parent," pp. 25–26.) The anomalous results in the above study are perhaps due to this measurement difficulty.

Finally, a study of junior high school boys reported mixed findings concerning resistance to temptation. (See W. Allinsmith, "Moral Standards: II. The Learning of Moral Standards," in D. R. Miller and G. E. Swanson, eds., *Inner Conflict and Defense* [New York:

types of discipline—physical punishment, threats of such punishment, and ridicule—are more likely to have this consequence, they argue, than the love-oriented forms of discipline. They explain their position in these words:

> Each of these [punitive techniques] seems likely when used by parents to have, to a considerable degree, the effect of setting up a tendency for the child to avoid the parents. Avoidance of the parents, because of anticipated pain or humiliation, should interfere to some extent with continued pursuit of the positive goal of attaining parental affection.[26]

The love-oriented types of discipline also make the child suffer, but these techniques, the argument runs, do this to a lesser extent than punitive techniques. If the child's need for parental love is diminished, the fear of losing that love—which is supposed to be central to the development of

---

Holt, 1960], pp. 141–76.) On the one hand, the investigator found high resistance to be associated with the extent to which the subjects' mothers gave explanations for obedience requests. The latter child-rearing procedure seems to have been equivalent to what other investigators call the use of reasoning by parents. This finding, therefore, accorded with the results of most of the studies cited above. On the other hand, there was no significant correlation between resistance to temptation and a typology of disciplinary measures based on three types—"corporal" punishment, "mixed" punishment, and "psychological" punishment.

Several things, however, vitiate this finding. Most studies consider each disciplinary technique separately and correlate each one with the dependent variable. By contrast, this investigation utilized a typology which classified mothers by the types of discipline they used most frequently. Unfortunately, the account given of how each type was defined and of how the materials were coded, is confusing. In one passage, it is said that only two kinds of discipline were considered in coding subjects. One was corporal discipline, as indicated by whipping and spanking. The other was "psychological" and took such forms as shaming the child, expressing disappointment, and appealing to his pride. Responses pertaining to two other kinds of discipline, scolding and the withholding of privileges, were ignored in coding subjects. This means that a subject could be placed in the psychological type despite the fact that his mother often resorted to such measures. Such a coding procedure could be a source of low validity since these measures are generally considered to belong to the punitive kind of discipline and have been found in other studies to relate to variables measuring ethicality in the same way as the use of physical punishment does.

A second difficulty of this study arises from the fact that one of the categories in the typology consists of the "mixed" kind of discipline. The author nowhere defines this type, nor does he specify what the coding procedures for it were.

We have reviewed several studies whose data are at variance with the relationships between disciplinary procedures and conscience that most studies show. Such discrepant findings, however, can, with perhaps a few exceptions, be adequately explained and do not appear really to invalidate the usual relationships that have been uncovered.

26. J. W. M. Whiting and I. L. Child, *Child Training and Personality* (New Haven: Yale University Press, 1953), p. 242.

conscience, according to Freud—cannot operate effectively in the child's psychic life.

Other interpretations of the role of discipline in the developing conscience have been suggested by M. L. Hoffman.[27] In discussing the "psychological" (i.e., nonpunitive) forms of discipline, he mentions the following factors as possibly accounting for the positive association of these forms with internalization: (1) this type of discipline may present "a model of self-restraint," or (2) it may give the child the knowledge necessary "for evaluating the rightness or wrongness of his act," or (3) it may create "unpleasant feelings" in the child about a misdeed. These are conjectures on Hoffman's part and have yet to be tested.

PARENTAL STRICTNESS

If severity of discipline in the sense of punitiveness favors the development of a weak conscience, severity in the sense of strictness appears to have the opposite effect. In their study of conscience among a sample of teen-agers, Peck and Havighurst examined the effects of "consistency in family life"—a factor analytic variable which, in part, tapped the degree to which the home life of the respondent was well regulated and orderly (as manifested, for example, by the existence of definite hours for meals, bedtime, and when to be in at night) and, in part, tapped the extent to which disciplinary procedures were consistent and predictable by the child. The investigators found that the consistency factor had high correlations with each of the variables designed to gauge the strength of conscience.[28]

A. Bandura's and R. H. Walters's research on juvenile delinquency also points to parental strictness as an important factor in the internalization of ethical views.[29] In this study the mothers of the "antisocial" group reported enforcing fewer rules about such things as the use of radio and television and were less likely to prohibit drinking and swearing than the mothers of the control group. They also placed less emphasis on obedience from their children. Both the fathers and the mothers of the control group said that they were more likely than the parents of the antisocial boys to have definite expectations about their child's performance in school and to put pressures on him to live up to these expectations. According to the interviews with the boys, moreover, the parents of the control group were more inclined to give their sons chores to perform around the house. All of these findings imply that the parents of the control group were distinguished, among other things, by a greater tendency to lay down certain

27. See Hoffman, "The Role of the Parent," pp. 30–31.

28. See Peck and Havighurst, *Psychology of Character Development*, pp. 103–8, 255–58.

29. See Bandura and Walters, *Adolescent Aggression*, pp. 195, 200–11.

standards and prohibitions and to demand conformity to these by their children.[30]

In the index of parental strictness employed here, one item simply asks the extent to which each parent "was strict toward his (her) children"; a second item deals with how "soft" each was in disciplinary matters. When run alone against Machiavellianism, this index yields a negative correlation (table 2.4). The higher the perceived strictness, the smaller the

TABLE 2.4
PERCENT HIGH ON MACHIAVELLIANISM BY PERCEIVED STRICTNESS OF PARENTS

	Father's Strictness		
	Low	*Medium*	*High*
% High Mach	34% (156)	32% (111)	28% (150)
	$\chi^2 = 1.339$; df = 2; $.75 > p > .50$.		
	Mother's Strictness		
	Low	*Medium*	*High*
% High Mach	37% (193)	29% (120)	27% (141)
	$\chi^2 = 4.131$; df = 2; $.25 > p > .10$.		
	Strictness, Same-Sex Parent		
	Low	*Medium*	*High*
% High Mach	34% (152)	30% (123)	29% (139)
	$\chi^2 = 1.094$; df = 2; $.75 > p > .50$.		

percentage that are Machiavellian. The correlations, however, are weak, a fact which, in part, reflects the positive association of the strictness variable with punitiveness. Consequently, in order to appreciate the importance of strictness, it is necessary to hold punitiveness constant. This we do in tables 2.5, 2.6, and 2.7. In each table, controlling for punitiveness results in a moderate improvement of the correlation between parental strictness and Machiavellianism.

The perceived disciplinary procedures of the parents, as measured by the strictness and punitiveness factors taken together, evidence a striking

30. Further data bearing on the role of the strictness factor is contained in Glueck and Glueck, *Unraveling Juvenile Delinquency*, p. 133.

TABLE 2.5

Percent High on Machiavellianism by Perceived Strictness and Punitiveness of Respondent's Father

Father's Punitiveness	*Father's Strictness*		
	Low	*Medium*	*High*
Low	26% (105)	25% (57)	18% (72)
High	51% (51)	39% (54)	37% (78)

A vs. B vs. C: $\chi^2 = 1.41$; df = 2; $.50 > p > .25$. D vs. E vs. F: $\chi^2 = 2.47$; df = 2; $.50 > p > .25$. A vs. D: $\chi^2 = 9.89$; df = 1; $p < .005$. B vs. E: $\chi^2 = 2.01$; df = 1; $.25 > p > .10$. C vs. F: $\chi^2 = 5.57$; df = 1; $.025 > p > .01$.

TABLE 2.6

Percent High on Machiavellianism by Perceived Strictness and Punitiveness of Respondent's Mother

Mother's Punitiveness	*Mother's Strictness*		
	Low	*Medium*	*High*
Low	28% (123)	21% (72)	16% (50)
High	54% (70)	42% (48)	33% (91)

A vs. B vs. C: $\chi^2 = 3.30$; df = 2; $.25 > p > .10$. D vs. E vs. F: $\chi^2 = 4.87$; df = 2; $.10 > p > .05$. A vs. D: $\chi^2 = 38.20$; df = 1; $p < .005$. B vs. E: $\chi^2 = 5.04$; df = 1; $.025 > p > .01$. C vs. F: $\chi^2 = 3.62$; df = 1; $.10 > p > .05$.

TABLE 2.7

Percent High on Machiavellianism by Perceived Strictness and Punitiveness of Parent of Same Sex

Punitiveness, Same-Sex Parent	*Strictness, Same-Sex Parent*		
	Low	*Medium*	*High*
Low	25% (94)	18% (61)	19% (63)
High	49% (57)	43% (58)	37% (75)

A vs. B vs. C: $\chi^2 = 1.77$; df = 2; $.50 > p > .25$. D vs. E vs. F: $\chi^2 = 2.02$; df = 2; $.50 > p > .25$. A vs. D: $\chi^2 = 6.96$; df = 1; $.01 > p > .005$. B vs. E: $\chi^2 = 6.69$; df = 1; $.01 > p > .005$. C vs. F: $\chi^2 = 4.27$; df = 1; $.05 > p > .025$.

correlation with Machiavellianism. If, in each table, one compares the upper, right-hand cell (high strictness, low punitiveness) with the lower, left-hand cell (low strictness, high punitiveness), the magnitude of the correlation becomes evident.

RAPPORT WITH SCHOOL AUTHORITIES

Freud comments in a number of passages that adults other than the parents influence the child's superego. Among such figures are the child's teachers and other school authorities.[31] He does not elaborate on the processes by which such influence operates, but if the internalization of parental standards reflects the degree of rapport between the child and the parents, it would seem that the influence of the school on the child's moral outlook would depend on the child's rapport with his teachers. The more a child feels accepted and approved of by the school, the more likely he will be to accept the moral standards which the school seeks to inculcate in pupils. Presumably school teachers, whose chief function is the socialization of the young, by and large present conventional moral values to their pupils, so that the influence of the school tends to be in a non-Machiavellian direction.

To measure the degree of rapport the respondent remembers as having existed between his teachers and him, we have constructed an index of two items. The first, in effect, asks whether he liked school or not. The second calls for the respondent's estimate of how much his teachers liked him. When cross-tabulated with Machiavellianism, the index yields a marked correlation (table 2.8). The greater the perceived rapport, the less likely is a respondent to be Machiavellian.

TABLE 2.8
MACHIAVELLIANISM BY PERCEIVED RAPPORT OF THE RESPONDENT WITH HIS SCHOOL DURING ADOLESCENCE

	Rapport with School		
Machiavellianism	*Low*	*Medium*	*High*
Low	23%	35%	39%
Medium	31	35	37
High	46	31	25
	100	100	100
	(93)	(203)	(166)

$\chi^2 = 36.552$; df = 6; $p < .005$.

Assuming that rapport with school authorities is a causal factor in the development of a person's moral outlook, its influence appears to be fairly

31. See, for example, Freud, *The Ego and the Id*, pp. 37, 48; and Freud, *New Introductory Lectures on Psychoanalysis*, pp. 92, 95.

important. This assumption, though, is problematic. The above correlation need not be due to the school's influence. It may be that, as adolescents, Machiavellians were relatively prone to engage in behavior—e.g., antisocial behavior—that had the effect of eliciting the disapproval of their teachers. If this were the case, the poor rapport reported by the Machiavellians would have been an effect, rather than a cause, of the failure to internalize moral norms. The data at hand unfortunately do not permit us to ascertain which interpretation is closer to the facts.

METHODS OF HANDLING AGGRESSION

According to Freudian theory, the turning inward of hostility accounts for guilt feelings, which in turn provide the mainspring for the operation of the superego. This gives rise to the hypothesis that the level of conscience is positively associated with the level of inwardly directed aggressiveness and negatively associated with the level of outwardly directed aggressiveness. The reason that the child turns his aggressiveness inward, the Freudian argument goes, is his fear of losing the parents' love if he directs it against them. A corollary is that if the parents are not loving and warmhearted to begin with, the child need have little fear, for there is little to lose. Hence a second hypothesis: the degree of parental love for the child influences whether his aggressive feelings are turned inward—taking such forms as guilt, inferiority feelings, and depression—or are directed outward in the form of hostility and anger at other persons. The greater the parental love, the more his aggression will be inwardly directed. The less the parental love, the more it will be directed outward.

The relevance of methods of handling aggression for the operation of conscience has been evidenced primarily in studies dealing with delinquency. Bandura and Walters found that the antisocial boys in their study were much less likely than the boys in the control group to experience guilt when they transgressed social norms.[32] In the Gluecks' research, data based on Rorschach tests indicated that the delinquents were comparatively lacking in masochism, that is, in the "tendency to suffer and to be dependent," which in psychoanalytic thinking reflects a turning inward of aggressive urges. The Rorschach data also indicated that a higher proportion of the delinquents than of the nondelinquents had "destructive-sadistic" trends —i.e., the tendency "to destroy, to hurt, and so on."[33]

MacKinnon's investigation of the violation of prohibitions in a problem-solving situation touched on methods of handling aggression.[34] Four weeks

32. See Bandura and Walters, *Adolescent Aggression*, pp. 287–90, 302–8.

33. See Glueck and Glueck, *Unraveling Juvenile Delinquency*, pp. 234–36.

34. See MacKinnon, "Violation of Prohibitions."

after the experiment the subjects were questioned about their reactions to the experimental situation. Only 25 percent of the violators indicated feelings of guilt at having cheated. By contrast, 84 percent of the nonviolators—when asked hypothetically how they would have reacted if they had cheated—stated that they would have felt guilty, conscience-stricken, ashamed, and so forth. Furthermore, a much greater proportion of the nonviolators indicated that they often had guilt feelings in everyday life. The investigator also collected data on outwardly directed aggressiveness. These revealed that a greater percentage of the violators than of the nonviolators vented anger by carping at the problems they were asked to solve. Also, the violators had a greater tendency to engage in activities that the investigator interpreted as signs of aggressive restlessness, such as kicking the leg of the table.

Several studies have found parental affection to be associated with the way in which a person deals with aggressive feelings. W. McCord and his associates selected a subsample of 174 protocols from the records of non-delinquent boys who had participated in the Cambridge-Somerville Youth Study of the 1930s.[35] Information concerning each boy and his family had been gathered over a period of years from various sources—teachers, counselors, physicians, social agencies, employers, etc. Using as indicators fist fighting, bullying of smaller children, destructive acts, verbal expressions of hostility, and other such behavior, the investigators measured how much overt aggression each boy had shown. They also had data on parental behavior, which they used to classify parents as affectionate or rejecting. It was found that the greater the amount of affection given by the parents, the less likely were the boys to be overtly aggressive.[36]

Finally, one investigation of male college students dealt with both the inwardly directed and the outwardly directed types of aggressiveness.[37] The subjects were classified as "Anger-In" or "Anger-Out" on the basis of the emotions they reported experiencing during participation in a series of experiments designed to induce stress. The Anger-Out subjects were those who said that they had feelings of anger toward the experimenter or the experimental situation. The Anger-In subjects reportedly experienced feelings of anger during the course of the experiments, but their anger was

35. See W. McCord, J. McCord, and A. Howard, "Familial Correlates of Aggression in Nondelinquent Male Children," *Journal of Abnormal and Social Psychology*, 62 (1961): 79–93.

36. Two investigations, in which R. R. Sears was the senior author, yielded similar results for preschool children. See Sears et al., *Identification and Child Rearing*, pp. 263, 527; and Sears et al., "Some Child-Rearing Antecedents of Aggression and Dependency in Young Children," *Genetic Psychology Monographs*, 47 (1953): 135–236.

37. See D. H. Funkenstein, S. H. King, and M. E. Drolette, *Mastery of Stress* (Cambridge, Mass.: Harvard University Press, 1957), pp. 32–37, 188–97.

wholly or mostly directed toward themselves. The two groups were distinguished by the different relations which they said they had had with their fathers. The Anger-Out group usually characterized their relations with their fathers as having been "hostile or strained and poor." The subjects exhibiting the Anger-In pattern, on the other hand, were more likely to describe relations with their fathers as having been "close and affectionate."

In order further to test Freud's ideas about the handling of aggressive feelings, we have formed two indices using items taken from the Edwards Personal Preference Schedule. Like the Machiavellian scale, the EPPS has a forced-choice format. Each item consists of two statements, and the respondent is required to check which of the two is more applicable to him or which more accurately describes him. One statement in each item is keyed to the variable the scale is meant to measure; the other is equivalent in "social desirability" but drawn from one of the other "needs" measured by the EPPS.

Based on items taken from the need Aggression scale of the EPPS, the first index we have constructed is meant to measure the extent to which a person's aggressive feelings are directed "outward" against other people, as distinct from being turned "inward" against himself. The wording of the items refers to hostile feelings and affect, not to the expression of aggression in overt behavior. The index deals with impulses such as those for "telling other people off when I disagree with them," "getting revenge when someone has insulted me," and "blaming others when things go wrong with me."

The second index utilizes items from the need Abasement scale of the EPPS. It refers to the propensity to turn one's aggressive feelings against oneself in the form of guilt, inferiority feelings, and depression. Some of the statements in the index read: "I feel that I am inferior to others in most respects," "I feel depressed by my own inability to handle various situations," "If I do something that is wrong, I feel that I should be punished for it."

The relationships of the above two indices to Machiavellianism are in accord with Freudian theory and with the results of previous studies. Table 2.9 deals with the aggression index, which is intended to measure the outward form of aggression. The higher a person is on aggression, the more likely he is to be Machiavellian.

The data bearing on inwardly directed aggression also lend support to the Freudian notions (table 2.10). Persons who are high on abasement are less inclined to be Machiavellian than persons who show little abasement. Although the correlation is not especially strong, it is in the expected direction.

If running abasement and aggression individually against Mach is one method of showing their relationship with Machiavellianism, another method

TABLE 2.9
MACHIAVELLIANISM BY AGGRESSION

Machiavellianism	*Aggression* Low	Medium	High
Low	38%	41%	20%
Medium	39	30	38
High	23	29	42
	100	100	100
	(129)	(212)	(138)

$\chi^2 = 14.095$; df = 4; $.01 > p > .005$.

TABLE 2.10
MACHIAVELLIANISM BY ABASEMENT

Machiavellianism	*Abasement* Low	Medium	High
Low	28%	38%	37%
Medium	32	34	38
High	40	28	25
	100	100	100
	(180)	(115)	(186)

$\chi^2 = 19.849$; df = 4; $p < .005$.

is to combine the two indices so as to form one variable. This we have done by simply subtracting each respondent's abasement score from his aggression score. The new index then presumably measures which trend predominates in the personality—the tendency to direct aggression outward or the tendency to direct it inward. If the calculated score is a positive number, the former is assumed to be more prominent. If it is a negative number, the latter would seem to predominate. If it is approximately equal to zero, the two tendencies are assumed to be balanced. This new index tends to ignore a person's absolute score on the components. A respondent, for example, who falls into the balanced category could do so either by having low and approximately equal scores on both variables or by having high and approximately equal scores on both variables. We have called this measure the index of balance between aggression and abasement.

When cross-tabulated with Machiavellianism, it yields noteworthy results. Table 2.11 shows that if outward aggression predominates in an individual's personality, he is more likely to be Machiavellian than if abasement predominates.

Although the data corroborate Freud's ideas on the relation between aggression and conscience, they are not consistent with some of his other

TABLE 2.11
MACHIAVELLIANISM BY INDEX OF BALANCE
BETWEEN AGGRESSION AND ABASEMENT

	Index of Balance		
Machiavellianism	*Abasement Predominant*	*Neither Predominant*	*Aggression Predominant*
Low	41%	38%	22%
Medium	36	35	32
High	23	27	46
	100	100	100
	(151)	(181)	(147)

$\chi^2 = 11.124$; df = 4; .05 > p > .025.

ideas. As we have seen, Freud suggests that the affectional relations between the child and the parent should influence a person's methods of handling aggression. When we examine the balance of abasement and aggression in relation to parental rapport, the correlation obtained is in the expected direction: outward aggression is more likely to be a prominent feature of an individual's personality if he had little rapport with the same-sex parent than if he had much rapport. The association, however, is a slight one.[38] Contrary to Freudian theory and unlike past investigations, the data fail to indicate that parental love toward the child exerts a conspicuous influence on the way he learns to handle aggression. We have no explanation for this discrepancy.

The findings here suggest that in whatever manner parental rapport may operate, its effects on Machiavellianism are not mediated by the balance of abasement and aggression. It follows that the rapport variable and the balance variable should make statistically independent contributions to Machiavellianism. This inference is confirmed by the data.

THE PROBLEM OF VALIDITY

The indices of parental characteristics used in this chapter are open to question. Recollections of childhood and adolescence have been asked of a sample that consists entirely of adults, many of whom are over forty years of age. In addition, some of the things we inquire about are nebulous. One item, for example, deals with the effectiveness of each parent in helping his children through emotional crises. Aside from the immensely complex judgment this item calls for, the connotations of its wording may vary among individuals. For many respondents, moreover, the matters asked about are

38. The tables for this finding and for the finding reported in the next paragraph are not shown here.

emotionally loaded and are, therefore, likely to be associated with distortions of memory and judgment.

The usual way out of such difficulties is for the investigator to assert that his interest is not in the childhood environment as such, but only in adult perceptions of that environment. This line of argument, however, seems unsatisfactory. If we devise measures dealing with the childhood environments of our respondents, it is because we are looking for the genesis of our dependent variable in these environments. To say that it does not matter whether the perceptions actually correlate with the phenomena they refer to, seems an evasion of the issue. Therefore, we propose to argue that the responses to the items about parents probably gauge—if only roughly—real differences in parental qualities and parental relations with their children.

The manner in which an individual's parents treated him is a salient part of his life—something to which he has most likely given some thought at one time or another. The items do not refer to isolated incidents from a person's past but to patterns of events which occurred many times over before the person arrived at adulthood and which presumably left a deep mark on him. An item about punitiveness does not ask about just one or a few incidents but about the manner in which each parent treated disciplinary problems over a period of many years. Furthermore, given that the respondent is an adult and that the events refer to the more or less distant past, it is possible that he can now view the events with a broader perspective. As a child or adolescent, the person may have been too involved to form any detached judgment. As an adult, he can take a more objective view since the experiences he has had can provide a yardstick for making evaluations. A person who idolized his parents too much as a child to see their less savory qualities may now be able to recognize these qualities for what they were. If, then, the validity of measures of parental behavior based on the responses of adult offspring can be questioned, plausible arguments can also be made for validity.[39]

In addition, there is one study relating Machiavellianism to parental characteristics as perceived by the respondent which was carried out on adolescents.[40] Amando de Miguel's sample consisted of 425 students ranging

39. Certainly such measures have ample precedent in the social sciences. See T. W. Adorno et al., *The Authoritarian Personality* (New York: Harper and Brothers, 1950), chap. 10; T. S. Langner and S. T. Michael, *Life Stress and Mental Health* (New York: Free Press, 1963), chaps. 9 and 10; W. L. Warner and J. C. Abegglen, *Big Business Leaders in America* (New York: Harper, 1955); E. Ellis, "Social Psychological Correlates of Upward Mobility Among Unmarried Career Women," *American Sociological Review*, 17 (1952):558–63; and G. Almond and S. Verba, *The Civic Culture* (Princeton, N.J.: Princeton University Press, 1963).

40. See Amando de Miguel, "Social Correlates of Machiavellianism: The Spanish Students," mimeographed paper (March 1964), pp. 21–23.

in age from sixteen to eighteen. Two of the items in his questionnaire that appear to be akin to the index of rapport with parents used here. These correlated negatively with Machiavellianism. Thus one of the present findings about the early family environment of the respondent has been replicated under conditions permitting greater confidence in the measurement of the independent variable. Other examples of how our findings on Machiavellianism accord with the results of previous researches on morality in children and adolescents were cited earlier in the chapter. This congruence is evidence that our indices tap, to some extent at least, actual variations in the childhood environments in which the respondents were reared.

A Final Word: The Composite Index of Parent Variables

The data presented above demonstrate that three of the four variables pertaining to the respondent's parents—the perceived Machiavellianism of the parents, the perceived rapport with the parents, and the perceived strictness of the parents—relate to Machiavellianism as would be expected on the basis of Freudian theory. Admittedly, the correlation of Machiavellianism with the fourth variable—the perceived punitiveness of the parents—could be interpreted as going contrary to Freudian theory. Nonetheless, all of the statistical relationships are consistent with the findings from previous research on ethical attitudes and behavior.

But perhaps these relationships are spurious, or perhaps one parental variable explains the relationship of another parental variable to Machiavellianism. To test for this possibility, we have run each of these variables against Machiavellianism while controlling for each of the others. Instituting such controls does not indicate spuriousness, nor does it suggest that the relationships involving each parental variable are mediated by any of the other parental variables.[41]

How much, then, of the variation in Machiavellianism is to be accounted for by the parental variables taken as an aggregate? In parametric statistics the coefficient of multiple correlation can be used to indicate how much of the variance in a dependent variable is accounted for by several variables together insofar as the latter are independent of each other. In cross-tabulation there is, strictly speaking, nothing corresponding to such a coefficient. A device sometimes used to accomplish the same purpose is a composite index, which is formed by aggregating several indices. Such an index is not intended to be unidimensional. Nevertheless, it does serve a useful function

41. A partial exception occurs when we run parental rapport and parental punitiveness simultaneously against Machiavellianism. The correlation of each of these variables with Mach is reduced when the other is controlled for, but the amount of reduction is minuscule.

by combining a number of variables whose collective relation to a dependent variable one wishes to measure.[42]

In order to gauge the combined effects of the parental variables, we have formed such a composite index. Since the procedures for calculating this index are described in the Appendix, the only remark necessary here is that a high score indicates that the perceived characteristics of a respondent's parents were such as to favor the development of Machiavellian attitudes.

TABLE 2.12
MACHIAVELLIANISM BY THE COMPOSITE INDEX OF PARENT VARIABLES

	Parent Index			
Machiavellianism	*Low*	*Medium-Low*	*Medium-High*	*High*
Low	46%	42%	30%	12%
Medium	36	33	36	32
High	19	25	34	57
	100	100	100	100
	(92)	(123)	(112)	(69)

$\chi^2 = 25.165$; df = 4; $p < .005$.

Table 2.12 gives the cross-tabulation of the composite index with Machiavellianism. The data show that the combination of parental variables has a much higher correlation with Machiavellianism than any one of these variables taken alone. We will have occasion in chapter 4 to return to this composite index in order to suggest how the family milieu interacts with the broader social environment to affect Machiavellianism.

42. An index of this sort is to be found in P. F. Lazarsfeld et al., *The People's Choice* (New York: Columbia University Press, 1948), pp. 26–27, 174–75. The researchers wished some measure of social background factors predisposing toward a Democratic or Republican vote. They accordingly based their index of political predisposition on the three social variables "with the best predictive value for vote"—religion, socio-economic status, and urban-versus-rural residence—despite the conceptually disparate nature of the component variables. In addition to providing a substitute for multiple correlation, this index served other useful functions. One was to show how social background factors, taken collectively, interacted with certain aspects of the political campaign to influence a person's voting intention. This permitted the researchers to compare the effects of background characteristics with the effects of the campaign. The composite index we have constructed here will be employed in an analogous fashion in a later chapter.

Another such measure is the Childhood-Adult Combined Stress Score in T. S. Langner and S. T. Michael, *Life Stress and Mental Health* (New York: Free Press, 1963), chap. 14. This is an aggregate measure of the various factors which are associated with psychiatric Il-health . By employing this index, the researchers were able to compare the combined effects of the stress variables with the effects of socioeconomic status in order to show that these two sets of factors operate independently of each other in relation to mental health.

CHAPTER 3

Sympathy and the Need for Social Approval

FREUDIAN THEORY posits a definite source of moral ideas (the parents); a limited, if not exactly specified, period of life during which superego formation takes place (childhood and possibly adolescence); and clearly drawn psychological mechanisms by which the person incorporates moral standards into his personality (identification, the fear of losing parental love, the turning inward of aggression). The writings of Charles H. Cooley are, in these respects, cast in a distinctly different mold.[1] Cooley eschews a focus on any single source of moral values. Nor is the formation of conscience, for him, confined to a given stage in an individual's life: there is, instead, a process of continual development. The single determinate element in his theory is the mechanism (the looking-glass self) by which conscience operates, but this is viewed as mediating a variety of influences.

In Freud's conception, moreover, the superego includes a code of moral standards that is crystallized in the personality by a certain period in an individual's life and thereafter remains relatively unchanged. Although Cooley recognizes that a person may develop a moral code, which, in turn, becomes independent of its original sources, he tends to underplay its role in the functioning of conscience. Instead, he emphasizes the ever present influence of social factors on moral life and the intrapsychic processes (sympathy and the need for social approval) which mediate this influence. For Cooley, one's sense of ethics is constantly changing: "The right never remains precisely the same two days in succession; but as soon as any particular state of right is achieved, the mental centre of gravity begins to move onward and away from it, so that we can hold our ground only by effecting a new adjustment."[2]

1. The major exposition of Cooley's theory is to be found in C. H. Cooley, *Human Nature and the Social Order* in *The Two Major Works of Charles H. Cooley* (Glencoe, Ill.: Free Press, 1956). G. H. Mead's theory is, in certain respects, similar to Cooley's. See G. H. Mead, *The Social Psychology of George Herbert Mead*, ed. A. Strauss (Chicago: University of Chicago Press, 1956), especially pt. 5.

2. Cooley, *Human Nature and the Social Order*, pp. 366–67.

Cooley's Theory of the Looking-Glass Self

Conscience, according to Cooley, is molded by the passions, sentiments, impulses, motivations, and interests of a given personality. A person's ethical judgment in a specific situation is a product of long deliberation by the mind and represents an attempt to reconcile these diverse and conflicting elements. "The mind is the theatre of conflict for an infinite number of impulses, variously originating, among which it is ever striving to produce some sort of unification or harmony." The balance which the mind finally strikes among all these elements determines one's sense of right.[3]

Though the elements entering into a moral decision are of diverse origin, Cooley's theory concentrates on one broad class of impulses—those arising out of sympathy. By this last term is meant the process of sharing in the thoughts and sentiments of other individuals. What Cooley is thinking of here is not simply an intellectual awareness of the other's reactions, but an emotional experiencing of his state of mind.[4] He thus employs *sympathy* in the same way as more recent authors often use the term *empathy*. The latter word, however, because of the measurement procedures commonly associated with it, has taken on connotations that we wish to avoid here. Consequently the term *sympathy* will be retained for the purposes of this discussion.

Another factor influencing conscience is the need for social approval. Cooley believes that the central motive of human behavior is the desire to maintain a high level of self-esteem. The strategy for accomplishing this varies with the individual—a fact that accounts for many basic differences in personality and life style. Nonetheless, self-esteem is ultimately dependent on the approval of others. Hence, the craving for such approval is a recurring theme in Cooley's writings.[5]

The influence of sympathetic impulses and of the need for social approval on conscience is to be understood, in Cooley's theory, in terms of the "looking-glass self."[6] There are three stages in the looking-glass process. First, one imagines how he—or anything pertaining to him, such as his behavior or his values—appears to another individual. Then he imagines this other person's judgment of this appearance. These first two stages involve sympathy. Finally, there is a response to this judgment with some kind of self-feeling, such as pride or mortification. If the individual imagines that the other person looks with favor upon his appearance, he may react with pride. If he believes that the other person is displeased, his reaction may be

3. See ibid., pp. 358–61, 374–75, 383.
4. See ibid., pp. 136, 395–96.
5. See, for example, ibid., p. 203.
6. See ibid., pp. 183–85.

one of shame. In this way, a person's attitudes and behavior are guided by the approval or disapproval he expects them to evoke in others.

The looking-glass self mediates the influence of other persons in several ways. For one thing, we look to certain persons as guides in solving moral problems and as sources of our moral standards. We adopt their standards and abide by them lest we incur their imagined displeasure by doing otherwise. Among the several kinds of guides discussed by Cooley is that of authority. Many people, for example, look to the church for rules and values by which to live. Others do not rely on any one source but draw upon many influences for values, which they then synthesize into their own unique moral system.[7]

A second manner in which the looking-glass self operates has to do with the image which a person thinks others have of him. A person typically thinks of himself in a particular way and seeks to obtain social validation for this self-image. He may picture himself as an upright, honest man. By behaving in accordance with his image in the eyes of others, he ensures their holding a socially favorable view of him. Acting in a contrary manner, on the other hand, would mean tarnishing this image and causing his associates to become disappointed in him. In seeking to maintain a good reputation among his fellows, a person adopts certain self-conceptions, which then become an effective force in regulating his behavior.[8]

Finally, the looking-glass self affects conscience insofar as it leads one to take account of the feelings and views of those who are affected by his conduct. Wrongdoing, from this perspective, stems from a person's failure to put himself into the shoes of the injured party. If the kidnapper could genuinely partake in the feelings of despair, anxiety, and fear with which the parents of his victim react to the crime, he would not have the heart to carry out his ugly deed.[9]

The first two ways in which the looking-glass self operates entail adopting the standards of given individuals or groups. In looking to a particular individual or group as a guide in moral matters, we *ipso facto* accept the standards of that individual or group. Seeking social esteem through living up to the image others have of us also implies that we assent to the moral values of these others. If people give approval for living up to a certain image, it is because that image is in accord with the moral standards of the group. A group that praises an individual for his honesty would not do so unless it placed a positive value on honesty.

In Cooley's theory, however, not just anybody's approval or disapproval matters to the individual. There are certain groups and persons whose

7. Ibid., p. 386.
8. See ibid., pp. 206, 385–88, 397.
9. See ibid., pp. 395–96.

opinion of his actions does not affect him, while the opinion of others decidedly does. The latter, to use a phrase coined after Cooley's time, are reference groups and individuals. An individual's reference group need not consist solely of persons with whom he has social relations; it may also consist of more distant individuals—the authors of his favorite books, characters in literary works, or persons he knew a long time ago. Unfortunately, Cooley has nothing explicit to say about what determines which individuals and groups shall become points of normative reference for a person.

Insofar as the looking-glass self operates through a reference group, the conscience that it fosters is not necessarily ethical from the standpoint of the wider society. Whether it is or not depends on the ethicality of the group's standards. A businessman who derives his moral values from a coterie of amoral, avaricious associates is not likely to see anything reprehensible in misrepresenting his products to the public. Thus deviance, according to Cooley, can often be explained by the fact that the norms of a person's reference group are deviant.[10]

Even though Cooley does not say so explicitly, the matter seems to be otherwise when the conscience comes into play through our imagining the thoughts and feelings of those whom we affect. For then a person's conduct does not—or does not so much—depend on the standards of these others. If A tricks B, B will be angry even though B's conscience ordinarily condones such trickery. A person may be entirely amoral in his outlook; yet when he himself is the victim of some transgression, he will become as indignant as if he believed in the violated norm. If so, imagining the reactions of the injured party to an injustice tends to restrain a person from unethical behavior independently of the moral values of the injured party.

In this respect, the looking-glass self is by itself sufficient to produce a socially acceptable functioning of conscience. But, as we have seen, it is not sufficient to do this insofar as it mediates the acceptance of the values of reference groups. Yet Cooley writes as though a deficiency in sympathy per se may account for "selfishness," "egotism," or "degeneracy." In one passage, he says that "the commonest and most obvious form of selfishness is perhaps the failure to subordinate sensual impulses to social feeling, and this, of course, results from the apathy of the imaginative impulses that ought to effect this subordination."[11]

This apparent contradiction, however, is not irresolvable. Cooley perhaps assumed that the reference groups of most individuals have norms that are in accord with those of the wider society. Therefore, although sympathy does not *have* to promote socially acceptable moral behavior, for most people it, in fact, does.

10. Ibid., p. 416.
11. Ibid., p. 214.

Another possible meaning that can be attributed to Cooley is that a socially acceptable moral outlook is by and large the product of social influences. He writes in one passage that "the idea that the right is social as opposed to sensual is, it seems to me, a sound one, if we mean by it that the mentally higher, more personal or imaginative impulses have on the whole far more weight in conscience than the more sensual."[12] In Cooley's terminology, "the mentally higher, more personal, or imaginative impulses" refer to elements in psychic functioning that are generated by sympathy and therefore reflect social influences. A person deficient in sympathy is *ipso facto* isolated from those social influences which foster the generally accepted ethical attitudes of a society; his impulses are solely of a sensual sort. Hence Cooley may be saying that although the person who is inclined to sympathy may be exposed to deviant influences, he is less likely to have a morally defective conscience than one who, by virtue of his lack of sympathy, is isolated from social influences.

The foregoing review of Cooley's ideas suggests a number of hypotheses, two of which have been tested with the present data. The first is that a person's ethicality varies with his ability to sympathize with others. The second is that his ethicality varies with the magnitude of his need for social approval.

Although the second proposition seems implicit in Cooley's writings, he himself might not agree with it. Unlike the tendency to sympathize, the need for social approval is not a variable in Cooley's conception. He treats this need as a constant, maintaining that all people are dependent on the good opinion of others: "no one can really stand alone."[13] What appears as less sensitivity to the opinions of others may be due, Cooley argues, to a less acute imagination of how others react to oneself, or it may indicate that the person is not dependent on the esteem of those in his immediate vicinity but relies on figures whom he supplies in his imagination. Nevertheless, this need appears as a conceptually distinct element in the process of the looking-glass self, and the present data, as well as the findings of others, suggest that it may fruitfully be thought of as a variable.

Previous Empirical Research

Any search for evidence bearing on the propositions gleaned from Cooley's writings has to contend with certain difficulties. There seem to be no pertinent studies of sympathy, as the term has been defined here. Research on role-taking ability might be considered relevant, but the latter variable, as we

12. Ibid., p. 378.
13. Ibid., p. 203.

argue in the next section, is fundamentally different from sympathy. A review of such research is consequently not appropriate here.

There are, on the other hand, studies concerning the need for social approval in relation to ethicality. The difficulty here is that all of these have methodological weaknesses. Nevertheless, lacking studies that employ sound procedures, we shall review those which exist.

A study by H. G. Gough employed the Socialization scale of the California Psychological Inventory, which had been explicitly developed, in part, on the basis of Mead's theory of the generalized other.[14] Although Gough did not use such terms, the best characterization of a major portion of the scale is that it measures the need for social approval. Some of the items read: "Before I do something, I try to consider how my friends will react to it." "I find it easy to 'drop' or 'break with' a friend." Since, however, most of the items refer to dimensions other than this need—so that the scale is not a pure measure of it—the study is unsatisfactory from our standpoint.

The correlates of the scale are nonetheless of some interest. The scale differentiated at a high level of significance between "more socialized" individuals (such as "best citizens" in high school and medical school applicants) and "less socialized" persons (such as high school pupils who were disciplinary problems, jail inmates, and delinquents). Among asocial individuals, the scale differentiated between those whose delinquent acts were more serious and those whose delinquent acts were less serious.

A second bit of evidence comes from a study of sociopathy by D. T. Lykken.[15] Sociopaths are generally defined by psychiatrists as criminally inclined deviants who are untrustworthy, insensitive to social demands, impulsive, and prone to poor judgment and shallow emotionality.[16] Lykken's investigation was based on a comparison of three groups: "primary" sociopaths, "neurotic" sociopaths, and normals. The author did not specify the differences between the first two groups; evidently the members of the second group had neurotic symptoms in addition to their sociopathy.

The three groups were given various instruments and procedures designed to measure anxiety. One of these was an ingenious paper-and-pencil

14. See H. G. Gough, "Theory and Measurement of Socialization," in T. R. Sarbin, ed., *Studies in Behavior Pathology* (New York: Holt, Rinehart and Winston, 1961), pp. 141–49; and D. R. Peterson, "The Identification of and Measurement of Predisposition Factors in Crime and Delinquency," *Journal of Consulting Psychology*, 16 (1952):207–12.

15. See D. T. Lykken, "A Study of Anxiety in the Sociopathic Personality," in Sarbin, ed., *Studies in Behavior Pathology*, pp. 149–54.

16. For a brief historical sketch of the concept of psychopathy, see H. G. Gough, "A Sociological Theory of Psychopathy," *American Journal of Sociology*, 53 (1948):359–66; and R. W. Ramsay et al., "Conscience Operation in a Normal Population," *Journal of the Canadian Psychiatric Association*, 11 (1966):80–90.

test developed by Lykken himself. (The Lykken Anxiety Scale is described below.) Even though Lykken conceptualized his instrument as measuring anxiety, one can plausibly argue that most of the items tap a sensitivity to social disapproval. If this study is not conclusive from our standpoint, it is because some of the items measure another dimension.

Lykken found that, when the three groups were compared on his scale, the normals made the highest score; the neurotic sociopaths, the next highest; and the primary sociopaths, the lowest. If our interpretation of the Lykken scale is correct, this finding implies that the sociopathic person has comparatively little concern with the good opinion of others.

Despite the methodological weaknesses of the above studies, they are instructive, for both point to the importance of the need for social approval as a factor in ethicality. This consistency is persuasive since these investigations employ different measures for both the independent and dependent variables. If, then, each of the studies has a flaw, the findings may nevertheless be indicative of genuine correlations between the variables.

Problems of Measurement

It is a truism of the social sciences that testing hypotheses requires being able to measure the relevant variables. In the case of sympathy and the need for social approval, however, measurement is problematic since—despite the profusion of scales in existence for measuring all sorts of personality variables—no satisfactory indices of these two variables have heretofore been developed.

THE MEASUREMENT OF SYMPATHY

In saying this, we are not overlooking the plethora of studies which have been done in the last few decades on a variable which, on the surface, appears closely related to the concept of sympathy.[17] This variable has been given different labels in the literature—"empathy," "role-taking ability," and "accuracy of person perception" being the most common. It refers to the ability to make judgments about the attitudes, behavior, test performance, personality characteristics, or some other such aspects of other persons.

The purpose of this kind of research ordinarily is to uncover the correlates of this ability. The individuals under study are frequently referred to as the judges; those about whom they are required to make judgments are called subjects. The usual procedure is to utilize subjects with whom the judges have a prior acquaintance or to set up a situation which permits the subjects to be

17. See R. Taft, "The Ability to Judge People," *Psychological Bulletin*, 52 (1955): 1–23, for a résumé of the literature in this area.

exposed to the judges. Such exposure may be achieved by showing the judges a film of the subjects or by having individuals meet together in groups for a number of sessions. When the research relies on group meetings, the same individuals normally act as both judges and subjects, each group member being asked to make judgments about every other member.

To measure empathic ability, the investigators have the judges make predictions about each subject's responses to personality or attitude questionnaires or self-ratings on various personality dimensions. These predictions are then compared to the actual responses or self-ratings of the subjects and the difference between the two is calculated for each item or dimension. The sum of the difference scores made by a given judge is taken as a measure of the judge's empathic ability.

This procedure was not possible in the present investigation, based, as it is, on survey methods. Since we viewed sympathy as a central concept in the study of Machiavellianism, we sought an alternative measure. As the exposition above showed, Cooley defines sympathy as the process of affectively sharing another person's thoughts and sentiments. If measures of role-taking ability, in fact, tap this process, they do so by gauging what is presumed to be an outcome of it—namely, the accuracy with which the judge is able to predict the attitudes or self-conceptions of the subject. Conceivably one could also measure the importance of sympathy in a person's psychic functioning by directly asking him whether he is sympathetic. In effect, one could ask the respondent: are you the kind of person who likes imagining how other people feel and think?

Social scientists use this procedure to measure other qualities of personality. To find out whether a person tends to project his aggressions against himself, they may take specific instances of self-aggression—whether the person feels guilty, has moods of depression, and so forth—and ask him whether each instance is descriptive of him.

One of the scales in the Edwards Personal Preference Schedule permits the same procedure with sympathy. The need Intraception scale deals with the inclination to analyze oneself and others psychologically. If the items referring to self-examination are omitted, most of the remaining items concern the proclivity for imaginatively placing oneself in the thoughts and feelings of other people. Some of the statements of the latter sort read: "I like to understand how my friends feel about the various problems they have to face"; "I like to put myself in someone else's place and to imagine how I would feel in the same situation." The present questionnaire contains seven such EPPS items, which have been aggregated to form a sympathy index.

A possible objection to such an index is that it is contaminated with social desirability. Since a preference for putting oneself in the other person's shoes and experiencing his emotions and thoughts is probably considered a desirable quality by most people, respondents might be wittingly or unwittingly prone to ascribe this quality to themselves even though such ascription would not be accurate. Admittedly, this is an important consideration. The forced-choice format of the EPPS, however, represents an attempt to overcome this difficulty. As with the aggression and abasement indices, which were described earlier, each item in the sympathy index consists of a pair of statements. One of the statements is keyed to the sympathy variable; the second is drawn from some random variable but is intended to have an equivalent, or nearly equivalent, rating on social desirability.

Although this index was originally adopted as a matter of necessity, it may have certain virtues that seem to be lacking in the usual procedures for measuring empathic ability. Considerable attention has been devoted in the journals to whether these procedures actually assess a sympathetic process. Several social scientists argue that accuracy in person perception may result from abilities and processes other than sympathy.[18]

One component of accuracy, for example, is knowledge of the cultural subgroup of which the subject is a member. If the judge knows that the subject is a college student, he may make predictions about the subject's responses to particular attitude items on the basis of his awareness of the relative frequency of the possible responses among college students. If the subject is typical of college students, the judge can achieve a high degree of accuracy without having sympathetically transposed himself into the subject's thoughts and feelings.

Another factor that may sometimes enhance accuracy is the tendency of the judge to project his own attitudes or feelings onto the subject. According to U. Bronfenbrenner and his associates, most judges attribute to others the responses that they themselves would make to a series of items.[19] A high role-taking score, then, may be the result of a fortuitous combination of circumstances—namely, the inclusion in a given study of judges who have

18. Our remarks on the nonsympathetic factors in role-taking accuracy are based primarily on the following sources: A. H. Hastorf and I. E. Bender, "A Caution Respecting Measurement of Empathic Ability," *Journal of Abnormal and Social Psychology*, 47 (1952): 574–76; L. J. Cronbach, "Processes Affecting Scores on 'Understanding of Others' and 'Assumed Similarity'," *Psychological Bulletin*, 52 (1955):177–93; N. L. Gage and L. J. Cronbach, "Conceptual and Methodological Problems in Interpersonal Perception," *Psychological Review*, 62 (1955):411–22; and G. Marwell, "Problems of Operational Definitions of 'Empathy,' 'Identification,' and Related Concepts," *Journal of Social Psychology*, 63 (1964):87–102.

19. See U. Bronfenbrenner et al., "The Measurement of Skill in Social Perception," in D. McClelland et al., eds., *Talent and Society* (Princeton, N.J.: Van Nostrand and Company, 1958), p. 35.

both a marked tendency to project and a strong resemblance to the subjects on those dimensions which they are judging.

Different role-taking tasks require different degrees of extrapolation from the behavior which the judge observes or is acquainted with, to the items to be predicted. If the judge is exposed to a film in which the subject expounds on his views of Governor Ronald Reagan, it will probably not require a high level of abstract reasoning for the judge to infer the subject's position on the liberalism-conservatism dimension. There is a direct link between the item to be predicted and the observed material. If, on the other hand, the judge is asked to rate a subject on certain personality variables, such as introversion or the need for autonomy, the items to be predicted may be many steps removed from the observed behavior. The judge must conceptualize each dimension; he must decide which clues in the observed materials are relevant to each dimension; he must consider several clues from different parts of the material, and so forth. Thus, depending on the nature of the perceptual task, the ability to make logical inferences may be a contributing factor of some importance to the accuracy of the predictions.

In view of the effect these factors may have on accuracy in role-taking tasks, a high accuracy score need not reflect a proclivity for sympathizing. Rosalind Dymond Cartwright, who at one time was an enthusiastic proponent of role-taking accuracy as an index of sympathy, has conceded this point. Using the term *empathy* in the way we have employed the term *sympathy*, she writes: "People might be empathic without being able to predict and might be able to predict accurately without the process being an empathic one. . . ."[20]

Since the items of the sympathy index refer directly to the process they are intended to measure rather than to a presumed outcome of that process, this index does not suffer from the weaknesses found in measures based on accuracy of person perception. Sympathy is not an ability but a process, and, for the purposes of measurement, it is the propensity for engaging in this process that counts. From this standpoint, the sympathy index may actually have greater validity than measures of role-taking ability.[21]

20. Rosalind Dymond Cartwright in a letter to A. Buchheimer, quoted in Buchheimer, "The Development of Ideas about Empathy," *Journal of Counseling Psychology*, 10 (1963): 66.

21. Indeed, there is some empirical evidence that predictive accuracy would be negatively correlated with the sympathy index. Chance and Meaders presented ninety-six undergraduate men with the task of predicting responses to personality scales after having heard tape recordings in which two subjects each spoke for twenty minutes. Each subject in a given pair had scored at opposite extremes on a personality scale. The investigators compared the personality characteristics of the eighteen most accurate judges with those of the eighteen least accurate judges. The finding of interest here was that the least accurate

A corollary of Cooley's theory, according to the burden of the present argument, is that Machiavellianism is inversely correlated with sympathy. It follows from the foregoing discussion that the relationship of Machiavellianism to the accuracy of person perception constitutes another question altogether. Relying on R. Taft's résumé of studies on the ability to judge personality, Christie contends that the existing evidence indicates that "the best . . . judges are characterized by a lack of warmth in interpersonal relations. . . . This seems to be a characteristic of high scorers on Mach Scales." On the basis of these observations, he conjectures that Machiavellians—or, at least, those who would score high on both the Likert and forced-choice variants of the Mach scale—are relatively better judges of personality than non-Machiavellians.[22] If, as has been argued above, person perception and sympathy are two distinct variables, Christie's arguments are not necessarily in conflict with our line of reasoning here.

Indeed, those who are deficient in conscience can be shrewd judges of others. D. Glazer observes that juvenile delinquents are impressively adept at "conning" people with subterfuges which require acumen in judging the attitudes of others and that survival in the insecure world of the delinquent depends on the ability to discern the attitudes of institutional guards and other nondelinquent figures.[23] This type of sensitivity, however, evidently differs from sympathy in that, even though the delinquent may accurately perceive the attitudes of others, he probably does not affectively experience these attitudes.

THE INDEX OF THE NEED FOR SOCIAL APPROVAL

As we saw above, it was desirable, in devising an index of sympathy, to adopt items from an already existing scale purporting to measure another personality variable. We have followed the same tack in measuring the need for social approval.

The index of this variable consists of items taken from the Lykken Anxiety Scale. This instrument is in forced-choice format with forty items, each

judges scored significantly higher on the need Intraception scale of the EPPS than the most accurate judges. Since the items for the sympathy index are taken from the Intraception scale, this finding suggests the possibility that the index is inversely associated with accuracy in person perception. See J. E. Chance and W. Meaders, "Needs and Interpersonal Perception," *Journal of Personality*, 28 (1960):206–9.

22. See R. Christie, "Impersonal Interpersonal Orientations and Behavior," pp. 23–25. The evidence presented in one study, incidentally, fails to support Christie's conjecture. See J. Danielian, "Psychological and Methodological Evaluation of the Components of Judging Accuracy," *Perceptual and Motor Skills*, 24 (1967): 1166–67.

23. See D. Glazer, "A Note on 'Differential Mediation of Social Perception as a Correlate of Social Adjustment,'" *Sociometry*, 20 (1957):156–60.

composed of two statements. One of the statements in each pair refers to an anxiety-provoking activity or event; the other describes an activity which is intended to be equally distasteful but not anxiety provoking. The respondent is asked to check which of the two activities or events in each pair he prefers. The statements keyed to anxiety are of two kinds: some refer to incidents of a frightening nature; others to incidents which would ordinarily elicit shame or embarrassment in a person. The latter type of statement appears to tap a sensitivity to social approval. One, for example, involves "being cursed by an old friend." Another incident is "walking into a room full of people, you stumble on a footstool and sprawl on the floor." A desire to avoid such incidents—as indicated by a respondent's checking the non-embarrassing alternatives in a series of items—can be assumed to reflect a concern for the good opinion of others. The index of the need for social approval employs ten items relating to incidents of the embarrassing sort.

The validity of the two indices intended to measure the looking-glass process cannot be conclusively demonstrated. Since both relate to inner psychic processes, there is no simple criterion against which the indices can be validated and no simple validating test for them. We can discern what they measure—their "meaning"—only by noting their correlations with a whole series of other variables. Their meaning is a matter of "construct validity," to use L. J. Cronbach's and P. E. Meehl's terminology.[24]

Consequently, acceptance of the validity of these two indices must, for the moment, be tentative, resting primarily on their face content. In addition, Lykken's findings with respect to sociopathy are consistent with the conceptualization of the index of the need for social approval offered here. If the argument above—that the Lykken Anxiety Scale is in large part a measure of the need for social approval—is correct and if those who are deficient in conscience do in fact have little need for social approval, one would expect sociopaths to make low scores on the Lykken scale. And this, indeed, is what they do.

This discussion will be resumed in chapter 7, where we will present data lending further support to the validity of the indices of the looking-glass self.

The Empirical Findings

The sympathy index yields a respectable association when cross-tabulated with Machiavellianism. As Cooley's theory suggests, highly sympathetic individuals are less likely to be Machiavellian than those who are lacking in

24. See L. J. Cronbach and P. E. Meehl, "Construct Validity in Psychological Tests," *Psychological Bulletin*, 52 (1955):281–302.

TABLE 3.1
MACHIAVELLIANISM BY THE SYMPATHY INDEX

	Sympathy		
Machiavellianism	*Low*	*Medium*	*High*
Low	22%	36%	44%
Medium	42	32	32
High	36	33	25
	100	100	100
	(135)	(199)	(147)

$\chi^2 = 16.596$; df = 4; $p < .005$.

sympathy. Table 3.1 gives the figures. The second element in the looking-glass process, the need for social approval, also shows a moderately negative correlation with Machiavellianism (table 3.2). The greater a respondent's sensitivity to the good opinion of others, the less Machiavellian he is inclined to be.

TABLE 3.2
MACHIAVELLIANISM BY THE NEED FOR SOCIAL APPROVAL

	Need for Approval		
Machiavellianism	*Low*	*Medium*	*High*
Low	29%	31%	43%
Medium	32	39	32
High	39	30	25
	100	100	100
	(153)	(174)	(152)

$\chi^2 = 11.760$; df = 4; $.025 > p > .01$.

Although both of the predictions derived from Cooley's theory of conscience are confirmed, the correlations are not exceptionally strong. The data, however, are not really indicative of the true relationships since each index, comprising only a part of the scale from which it comes, is lacking in optimal reliability. The need Intraception scale of the EPPS, with its twenty-eight items has a split-half reliability of .79;[25] our sympathy index, employing seven of the intraception items, has a reliability of only .46. The same is true of the index of the need for social approval. The Lykken Anxiety Scale, from which the items for the index are taken, has a split-half reliability of approximately .70 for "normal" subjects and is forty items in length.[26]

25. See A. L. Edwards, *Manual for the Edwards Personal Preference Schedule* (New York: Psychological Corporation, 1959), p. 19.

26. David T. Lykken in a personal communication to this writer, May, 1963.

By contrast, the index used here is based on only ten items with a reliability of .46. Despite the relative unreliability of our measures, the correlations are of respectable magnitude. This suggests that the amount of the variation in Machiavellianism accounted for by sympathy and by the need for social approval is actually much greater than is indicated by tables 3.1 and 3.2.

Moreover, to run each of the two variables separately against Machiavellianism does not do justice to Cooley's theory. Sympathy and the need for social approval do not, according to this theory, operate independently of each other; they are part of a single process—the looking-glass self. If so, it seems permissible to combine them into a single variable. This we have done by summing each respondent's scores on the two variables (after making certain adjustments as described in the Appendix). The new index is labeled the Looking-Glass Process.

To score high on it, a respondent has to be relatively high on both of the component variables. A low score, on the other hand, means that he is relatively low on both variables. A medium score can reflect a medium score on the two components or a relatively high score on one in conjunction with a relatively low score on the other. The index is thus a composite measure.

Table 3.3 gives the cross-tabulation of this index with Machiavellianism. The data suggest a strong inverse correlation. The more important the looking-glass process is in an individual's personality, the less likely is he to be Machiavellian.

TABLE 3.3
MACHIAVELLIANISM BY THE LOOKING-GLASS PROCESS

	Looking-Glass Process			
Machiavellianism	*Low*	*Medium-Low*	*Medium-High*	*High*
Low	21%	32%	33%	48%
Medium	38	36	33	33
Low	41	32	34	19
	100	100	100	100
	(111)	(115)	(123)	(130)

$\chi^2 = 27.16$; df = 6; $p < .005$.

AN UNRESOLVED PUZZLE

In conclusion, both elements of the looking-glass self—sympathy and the need for social approval—correlate with Machiavellianism, as the hypotheses derived from Cooley's theory predict. Yet our data are also, in large part, consistent with Freud's theory of the superego, which, as we saw at the outset of this chapter, differs in several critical respects from Cooley's. Perhaps the most perplexing problem in this study has been how to resolve the differences between the two theories. In seeking a solution to this problem, we have tried linking the variables from the two theories in a number of ways. We explored the possibility, for example, that sympathy and the need for social approval are a function of variations in the respondent's family milieu as a child. We also asked whether sensitivity to social approval might not reflect a tendency toward abasement. Since neither of these tacks—nor any of the others that we tried—led to a satisfactory resolution of the intellectual puzzle, no reconciliation of the two theories has been accomplished.

CHAPTER 4

Solidarity as a Set of Independent Variables

Theoretical Perspectives on Solidarity

TOENNIES'S THEORY OF *Gemeinschaft* AND *Gesellschaft*

THE FINAL BODY of theory to be discussed has a more macrosociological perspective than either of the previous two. If Freud concentrates on parental influences on the superego and Cooley on the role of the looking-glass self and reference groups in the functioning of conscience, Ferdinand Toennies's stress is on the moral outlook of the individual in relation to the solidarity of the group or society.[1] Solidarity is implicit in his typology of *Gemeinschaft* and *Gesellschaft*, two terms which stand for different kinds of interpersonal relations and different kinds of social system.

In *Gesellschaft*, the type in which solidarity is lacking, everyone is "by himself and isolated," "essentially separated" from everyone else. "Mutual familiar relationships" are absent. There is a stress on privacy: the "spheres of activity and power are sharply separated, so that everybody refuses to everyone else contact with and admittance to his sphere." The prototype for social relations is barter and exchange; "nobody wants to grant and produce anything for another individual . . . if it be not in exchange for a gift or labor equivalent that he considers at least equal to what he has given." Interpersonal ties are permeated by self-seeking motives, each individual striving "for that which is to his own advantage" and cooperating with others "only insofar as and as long as they can further his interest." The result is that tension and "potential hostility or latent war" are common.[2]

In place of genuine and close friendships, *Gesellschaft* substitutes "conventional society life." Toennies acidly depicts how informal social ties of the *Gesellschaft* sort parallel relationships in the market place.

> The supreme rule is politeness. It consists of an exchange of words and courtesies in which everyone seems to be present for the good of everyone else . . . whereas in reality everyone is thinking of himself and trying to bring to the fore his

1. See F. Toennies, *Community and Society*, trans. Charles P. Loomis (East Lansing: Michigan State University Press, 1957).

2. See ibid., pp. 64–65, 76.

> importance and advantages in competition with others. For everything pleasant which someone does for someone else, he expects, even demands, at least an equivalent. He weighs exactly his service, flatteries, presents, and so on, to determine whether they will bring about the desired result.[3]

On the macrosocietal level, *Gesellschaft* finds its strongest expression in capitalism. Each individual tries to maximize his profits or income, while minimizing his expenditure of money or labor. In the ensuing conflicts of interest, the "commercial and business people race with each other on many sprinting tracks, as it were, trying each to get the better of the other. . . ." Capitalist society is also characterized by an "always widening hiatus" between the wealth of the bourgeois class and the poverty of the mass of the people.[4]

If *Gesellschaft* epitomizes the absence of solidarity, *Gemeinschaft* clearly represents a highly solidary type. It is distinguished by three characteristics: (1) an attitude of "love" among persons, (2) mutual "understanding" and consensus with respect to values and attitudes, and (3) proximity of dwellings and a strong, organized communal life.[5] It has different attributes, depending on the social relationship or society being described. Among kin, for example, *Gemeinschaft* connotes that "we are intimate, that we affirm each other's existence, that ties exist between us, that we know each other and to a certain extent are sympathetic toward each other, trusting and wishing each other well." Also involved at the kinship level are similarity in attitudes and the mutual recognition of "rights" and "duties."[6]

At the level of a locality or village, *Gemeinschaft* reflects a proximity of dwellings and agricultural holdings and the communal ownership of land. As a result of these characteristics, there is "inurement to and intimate knowledge of one another, . . . cooperation in labor, order, and management," and common religious observance.[7]

In a social collective, such as a caste or a racial group, *Gemeinschaft* is present insofar as the members regard the collective "as a gift of nature or created by a supernatural will." An example given by Toennies is the Indian caste system. The caste "has the same significance as a large family." One inherits his vocation and his social rank from his parents. The system is sanctioned by religion, and the onerousness which the members may feel "is lightened by the recognition that it cannot be changed."[8]

Corresponding to the sociological types in Toennies's theory is a typology of "wills." Although, strictly speaking, "will" is intended as a volitional concept, it nevertheless has to do with aspects of the personality other than

3. Ibid., p. 78.
4. See ibid., pp. 76–78, 258–59.
5. See ibid., p. 48.
6. See ibid., pp. 250–51.
7. See ibid., p. 43.
8. See ibid., p. 255.

volition, and it refers, among other things, to the moral outlook of an individual. The two types of will, according to Toennies, are natural will and rational will. The latter prevails in *Gesellschaft.*

Toennies defines rational will as volition in which thinking predominates and is "the directing agent." The individual with this type of will evaluates his actions strictly in terms of their efficiency for achieving his ends. The aims of such an individual tend to be of a material and worldly nature; among them are "pleasure, advantage, happiness."[9] This will culminates in a mentality which views life as "a business . . . with the definite end or view of attaining an imaginary happiness as its ultimate purpose."[10]

The stress on rationality and material values leads to an instrumental orientation in which other individuals are viewed as means for realizing one's objectives.[11] From this follows an amoral, manipulative outlook. The person of rational will does not hesitate to show "emotions contrary to real ones" or to conceal his objectives. He employs trickery and fraud when it is expedient to do so. Toennies aptly expresses the attitude of such a person in these words: "A false coin or an adulterated commodity and, in general, lies and make-believe, have, if they produce the same results, . . . the same value as the genuine article or the true word or the natural conduct."[12]

The second type of will, the natural will, is associated with *Gemeinschaft.* Much less distinctly drawn in Toennies's writing, it seems to be almost a residual category, encompassing everything which rational will is not. As such, it is not as unified a concept.

If the behavior of the rationally willed person reflects consciously sought after, egoistic motives, conduct associated with the natural will stems from likes and dislikes, from emotions such as love and hate, from habituation, or from a sense of duty. Such conduct is, in the words of one commentator, "controlled by love, understanding, customs, religion, folkways, and mores."[13] "Direct, naïve, and therefore emotional," naturally willed behavior has an uncalculating, spontaneous flavor.[14]

This spontaneity implies that other individuals are viewed as ends in themselves. The individual with a natural will does not use people. Characteristically he identifies with them. His motives "take the form of satisfying [the volition and desires] . . . of another individual, others, or whole groups." Toennies likens this attitude to a mother's love for her baby "from whom she does not expect or require anything as long as he has not reached the age of reason."[15]

9. See ibid., pp. 126–28.
10. Ibid., p. 144. Also see pp. 104, 120–23, 247, 252.
11. See ibid., p. 130.
12. See ibid., pp. 124, 131, 165.
13. See Charles P. Loomis, "Introduction," in ibid., p. 6.
14. See ibid., pp. 248–49.
15. See ibid., pp. 244–45.

One particularly influential element in the natural will is the sense of shame, which manifests itself in the disapproval which one feels toward himself, or which his associates express toward him, when he violates the ethical norms of society. Shame is the means by which conscience effectively regulates a person's conduct. The natural will, then, is associated with a highly developed conscience and a traditional sense of ethics.[16]

Since Toennies's writing is often verbose and obscure, it is not always easy to interpret precisely what he means. Just how the typology of wills is related to the sociological types is, for example, ambiguous. Their relationship seems to be a matter of definition. Thus Toennies writes, "I call all kinds of association in which natural will predominates *Gemeinschaft*, all those which are formed and fundamentally conditioned by rational will, *Gesellschaft*." But the phraseology here also suggests that will is thought of as an independent variable. If so, Toennies may be arguing that the modal personality characteristics of a group or society, as expressed in the most prevalent type of will, determine the character of social relations.[17]

In another passage, though, Toennies explicitly contends that the causal nexus runs in the other direction, that societal types mold the will of individuals: "*Gemeinschaft* develops and fosters natural will . . . and binds and hinders rational will." *Gesellschaft*, on the other hand, "requires and furthers [rational will], even makes its unscrupulous use in competition into a condition of the maintenance of the individual. . . ." It may be that Toennies conceives of the two typologies as exerting a mutual influence on each other, each operating as both cause and effect.[18]

Imprecision is also reflected in an apparent overlapping of the two typologies. One of the distinguishing features of *Gemeinschaft*, for instance, is that the members of a group "love" each other. An element in the natural will, however, is a noninstrumental attitude toward other people. Thus *Gemeinschaft* and natural will seem to have similar, if not identical, elements as parts of their conceptualization.

An additional problem is that Toennies's discussion is so loose that one cannot readily tell which elements are part of the definition of each concept and which are hypothesized as correlates. A case in point is the consensus of values and attitudes among the members of a group that he refers to in his exposition of *Gemeinschaft*. In some passages, this appears to be a component of the societal concept; in others, it could be interpreted as a correlate.

Despite an absence of the sort of precision which present-day social scientists expect of a theory, Toennies's writings are fruitful insofar as they direct attention to the link between the solidarity of a group or society and the moral outlook of its members.

16. See ibid., pp. 159–61. 17. Ibid., p. 249. 18. See ibid., pp. 169–70.

SOROKIN'S MODALITIES OF SOCIAL INTERACTION

In order to employ the concept of solidarity in a more systematic manner, it is useful to have a formal definition of the concept. We are fortunate in that one of the outstanding sociologists of our time has given considerable thought and empirical work to evolving what are, in effect, the elements of such a definition. Although Pitirim A. Sorokin does not use the term "solidarity," the dimensions he employs for characterizing social relationships provide valuable tools for defining the term. These dimensions represent a conceptual refinement of centuries of social thought, and they serve as the basis for Sorokin's typology of social systems, which has proved its empirical worth in the interpretation of the history of European social institutions.[19]

Four of Sorokin's dimensions are relevant to the present discussion. The first, extensity refers to "the proportion of the activities and psychological experiences involved in interaction out of the sum total of the activities and psychological experiences of which the person's whole life process consists." An example of a relationship wide-ranging in extensity is that of an infant to his mother. As Sorokin points out, "sleep, feeding, clothing, bedding, most of the baby's actions and feelings, are dependent upon the mother." By contrast, the relationship of a butcher to a housewife is usually limited to the buying and selling of meat; only a small sector of the life of either party comes into play.[20]

Sorokin does not explicitly define the second dimension, that of intensity. The illustrations he gives, however, indicate that it refers primarily to the strength of affect which each party feels toward the other and to the extent to which each party is psychologically affected by the actions of the other. The relationship of a religious teacher to his pupils may be such "that every word of the teacher will be accepted as the Gospel"; or at the other extreme, "the words and teachings of the preacher will be of little influence."[21]

The duration of a relationship, the third dimension, is simply the length of time that the relationship has existed.[22]

Finally, the direction of interaction has to do with the degree of concord existing in a relationship. In a solidary relationship, "the aspirations and respective efforts of one party concur with the aspirations and efforts of the other party." When the desires and activities of the parties conflict, the association is an antagonistic one. A social bond may consist of a mixture of solidary and antagonistic elements.

Although Sorokin's definition of solidary direction is based on the amount

19. See P. A. Sorokin, *Social and Cultural Dynamics* (New York: American Book Company, 1937), vol. 3, chaps. 1–3.

20. See ibid., pp. 6–9. 21. See ibid., pp. 9–11. 22. See ibid., pp. 11–15.

of friction existing in a relationship, his discussion suggests that he is equally concerned with a dimension such as the collectivity versus self-orientation of Tolcott Parsons's pattern variables. The latter refers to whether a person's behavior is guided by the welfare of the collective or by self-interest. Even though a relationship is solidary in direction, the motives of the participants may nevertheless be self-seeking.[23]

The type of social interaction that characterizes most institutions in contemporary industrial society, Sorokin calls contractualism. Among its essential features is a restricted extensity: social interaction tends to be "segmentalized," each relationship involving only a small sector of a person's life. Also, social relations are of limited duration or, when covering an extended time period, the duration is specified in a contract. Although interaction is by and large solidary in direction, it is nonetheless based on the egoistic advantage that each party hopes to gain. A final characteristic of contractualism is an intensity that is limited by virtue of its being weak or, if strong, confined to no more than a few areas of a person's life. Contractualism, as thus defined, seems to be the epitome of an unsolidary social system.[24]

Sorokin's familistic type serves as the locus for a high level of solidarity. This type is characterized as all-embracing in extensity; high in intensity; extended in duration; and solidary in direction (with the concord of the participants based on altruistic motives).[25]

In measurement, the ideal is to obtain indicators for each component of a variable. This, however, is not always feasible and has not been possible in the present research. Nevertheless, the specification of the components of a complex concept such as solidarity serves a useful function inasmuch as it enables us more easily to assess the adequacy of the measures we do have. The analysis below, for example, employs the population of a locale as an indicator of solidarity. Although this indicator does not refer directly to any of the component dimensions, we are able to cite several students of urbanism who contend that these dimensions vary with the size of a community and that size is therefore a valid measure.

Previous Research on Solidarity and Ethicality

In examining the empirical evidence bearing upon the relationship between solidarity and moral outlook or adherence to moral norms, one notes that the

23. See ibid., pp. 15–18.

24. See ibid., pp. 30–35.

25. See ibid., pp. 24–30. Sorokin's theory contains a third type, the compulsory type, but this has little relevance for our present purposes and has therefore been ignored in this discussion.

indicators of solidarity vary from one study to the next. Some may not be the best measures of the concept as formally defined here. Nevertheless, we have had to make the best of whatever data are available.

One of the areas of life in which Durkheim looked for measures of social integration was religion. He regarded Roman Catholicism as having greater cohesion than Protestantism since it leaves much less freedom to the individual in matters of doctrine and since its regulation of the individual's life covers a larger area.[26] Miller cross-tabulated the Machiavellian scale with religious preference for a sample of students drawn from eight medical schools. His data indicated that Protestants were more Machiavellian than Catholics—a finding that is consistent with Durkheim's argument that Protestants have less social integration than Catholics.[27]

Another indicator of solidarity would appear to be the size of a social unit. R. K. Goldsen and her associates found that cheating among college students varied directly with the number of students enrolled in the school.[28]

Several studies have used the degree of social and cultural homogeneity and the rate of residential mobility existing in an area as independent variables. The first is R. C. Angell's work on the moral integration of cities. To measure integration, he employed an index combining the crime rate with the amount of money given for social welfare activities (adjusted for the standard of living of the city). In a study of a large number of urban communities in the United States, the strongest negative correlates of moral integration were residential mobility and social heterogeneity. The multiple correlation of these two variables with the dependent variable was .79; the

26. See E. Durkheim, *Suicide*, trans. J. A. Spaulding and G. Simpson (Glencoe, Ill.: Free Press, 1960), bk. 2, chaps. 2 and 3.

27. Cited in R. Christie, "Impersonal Interpersonal Orientations and Behavior," p. 11. One finding of Miller's, however, conflicts with Durkheim's contention. Durkheim assumed that Judaism is more integrated socially than either Catholicism or Protestantism. On this basis, Jewish students should have a lower Machiavellian score than the students affiliated with the other two religions. Actually their score was higher. We think that this discrepancy can be explained in terms of the social transformation that the Jews have undergone since Durkheim's time. He based his assumption of the greater cohesion of the Jews on their enforced residential segregation and on the discrimination against them. Today in the United States these conditions no longer obtain to the extent that they once did. Moreover, there is no indication that Miller controlled for degree of urbanization of residence in his comparison of the three religious groups. It is likely that a higher proportion of Jews than of the other two religious groups grew up in highly urbanized areas. And degree of urbanization, as we shall demonstrate below, is correlated with Machiavellianism. For these reasons, we do not think that the relatively high score of the Jewish students conflicts with the hypothesized negative correlation between social solidarity and commitment to moral norms.

28. See R. K. Goldsen et al., *What College Students Think* (Princeton, N.J.: D. Van Nostrand, 1960), pp. 74–80.

coefficient was increased only negligibly by the addition of other variables.[29]

In an ecological study of juvenile delinquency in Baltimore, the only variables that continued to be significant in the prediction of the delinquency rate when other variables were controlled, were the degree of home-ownership and the degree of concentration of Negroes in an area. The author, B. Lander, regarded home-ownership as an index of stability, by which he apparently meant a low rate of residential mobility. In reference to the second variable, it was not a high concentration of Negroes as such that gave rise to a high delinquency rate. What was important was the mixture of Negroes and whites in a neighborhood, that is, social heterogeneity. This was implied in the decline in delinquency rate that occurred when the concentration of Negroes in an area passed a certain point.[30]

In an analysis of New World communities that were not integrated culturally or socially with their respective national systems, W. J. Goode examined the relation of illegitimacy rates to the extent to which communities were internally integrated. The indicators that he used for internal integration make it evident that it is akin to social solidarity as we are using the term here. Thus some of his indicators were the number of the young adults in a village who were attracted to city life and ways, and the proportion of the village that participated in ceremonies. In a table embodying villages that have been the object of community studies by anthropologists, Goode showed that internal integration was negatively correlated with illegitimacy rates.[31]

Finally, one can regard the degree of industrialization of an area as a measure of solidarity. A telling piece of evidence based on this measure comes from a study by de Miguel. He administered Mach V (the forced-choice variant of the Machiavellian scale) to 425 late adolescent *preuniversitario* students in Spain. The schools from which the sample was drawn were located in different provinces, which varied in the degree of their industrial development as measured by the male literacy rate. De Miguel found that Machiavellianism had a positive correlation with the industrialization of the province.[32]

29. See R. C. Angell, *The Moral Integration of American Cities* (Chicago: University of Chicago Press, 1951), chaps. 2 and 3.

30. See B. Lander, *Towards an Understanding of Juvenile Delinquency* (New York: Columbia University Press, 1954).

31. See W. J. Goode, "Illegitimacy, Anomie, and Cultural Penetration," *American Sociological Review*, 26 (1961):922–25.

32. See Amando de Miguel, "Social Correlates of Machiavellianism: The Spanish Students," mimeographed paper (March 1964).

The Results of the Present Investigation

Although previous research seemed to demonstrate the utility of solidarity as as explanatory concept, our own efforts to employ this concept initially met with considerable frustration. In the end, however, this concept yielded valuable results.

THE CHARACTERISTICS OF FRIENDSHIP TIES

Empirical research on primary social relations has generally measured the intensity of friendship by the frequency with which a person sees his friends. Although frequency is a legitimate variable that perhaps correlates with any independent measure of intensity that can be devised, it is nevertheless not the same thing as the "intimacy" or solidarity of a person's relations with his primary associates. Comparatively little attention, according to Robin Williams, Jr., has been paid to the latter variables.[33] In designing the present research, we felt that distinguishing the closeness of friendship ties from the frequency of visiting might prove fruitful. We have therefore developed independent measures for each.

In forming the index of frequency, we have relied on questionnaire items which ask "how often . . . do you get together socially" with each of three categories of persons—neighbors, fellow employees, and other acquaintances. An overall measure has been arrived at by aggregating the responses for the three categories.

The other measure, the index of the intimacy of friendship ties, is based on a section of the questionnaire in which the respondent is asked to list "the *five* persons (or married couples) *not related* to you, *whom you know best*." The respondent, in effect, gives five replies to each item, one for each of the friends listed. One item, for example, reads, "You know the immediate family of this person well." A response consists of placing a check mark under the name of each friend to whom the statement is applicable.

Four dimensions have been employed in constructing the intimacy index. The first three are taken from Sorokin's modalities of social interaction. These are the dimensions of intensity, extensity, and duration. One of the items intended to tap intensity asks if the respondent "would feel badly if you happened to lose touch" with each friend. The extensity item inquires about the range of topics the respondent talks about when he is with each friend.

33. See R. M. Williams, Jr., "Friendship and Social Values in a Suburban Community: An Exploratory Study," *Pacific Sociological Review*, 2 (1959):5. For another discussion that, in its own way, centers on closeness of primary relations, as distinct from the mere frequency of interaction, see B. N. Adams, "Interaction Theory and Social Network," *Sociometry*, 30 (1967):64–78.

To measure the duration component, we have calculated the mean percent of the respondent's life he has known the five friends listed. A fourth type of item deals with the extent to which the respondent knows the other primary associates of each friend and thus gauges the interconnectedness of the respondent's social circle.[34]

That the intimacy and the frequency variables are not the same is suggested by their cross-tabulation (table 4.1). Although they have a fairly high correlation with each other, the correlation is hardly strong enough for the two variables to be considered as alternative ways of measuring the same concept. Indeed, if one looks only at the three highest categories of the

TABLE 4.1
INTIMACY OF FRIENDSHIP TIES BY FREQUENCY OF SEEING FRIENDS

	Intimacy			
Frequency	*Low*	*Medium-Low*	*Medium-High*	*High*
Low	45%	25%	13%	16%
Medium	37	46	47	47
High	19	29	40	37
	100	100	100	100
	(112)	(113)	(105)	(129)

$\chi^2 = 38.748$; df = 6; $p < .005$.

intimacy variable, there is little correlation. It is primarily the tendency of respondents in the lowest intimacy category to see friends rarely that accounts for the statistical association in the table. Hence, a large number of respondents whose friendship ties are comparatively lacking in intimacy nonetheless get together with friends fairly often.

Running each of the two variables against Machiavellianism provides further evidence that they are conceptually different. Frequency has a slight positive association with Machiavellianism: the more often a person gets together socially with friends and acquaintances, the more likely he is to be Machiavellian.[35] Intimacy, on the other hand, correlates with Machiavellianism in the opposite direction (table 4.2). The two variables have a modest negative association, so that individuals with close friendship ties are less inclined to be Machiavellian than individuals with loose friendship

34. The items comprising the intimacy index are listed in the Appendix. Williams's work on friendship proved a valuable source of suggestions for item formulation. See R. M. Williams, Jr., "Friendship and Social Values in a Suburban Community," mimeographed (Department of Sociology, University of Oregon, 1956). In addition to containing the questionnaire for the study, this work gives a more comprehensive account of the research reported in the article which we cited in note 33 above.

35. The relevant table is not shown here.

TABLE 4.2
MACHIAVELLIANISM BY THE INTIMACY OF FRIENDSHIP TIES

	Intimacy			
Machiavellianism	*Low*	*Medium-Low*	*Medium-High*	*High*
Low	29%	34%	33%	43%
Medium	39	30	36	29
High	32	37	31	28
	100	100	100	100
	(112)	(115)	(106)	(129)

$\chi^2 = 7.543$; df = 6; .50 > p > .25.

ties. If the intimacy variable and the frequency variable were interchangeable, one would expect them to correlate in the same way with a third variable. Since the correlations of the two variables with Machiavellianism have opposite signs, one can infer that they are measuring different things.

The opposite directions of the two correlations, taken with the positive association of intimacy and frequency with each other, tell us something else: we cannot discern how the intimacy of a person's friendship ties is actually related to Machiavellianism unless we hold frequency constant. We have therefore divided the sample in two, one part consisting of respondents who see their friends and acquaintances relatively often, the other of respondents who engage in social visiting with less frequency. Table 4.3

TABLE 4.3
MACHIAVELLIANISM BY THE INTIMACY OF FRIENDSHIP TIES

	Intimacy			
Machiavellianism	*Low*	*Medium-Low*	*Medium-High*	*High*
For Respondents Who See Friends with Little Frequency				
Low	35%	39%	42%	58%
Medium	39	27	36	16
High	26	34	21	26
	100	100	100	100
	(69)	(41)	(33)	(31)
	$\chi^2 = 8.2145$; df = 6; .25 > p > .10.			
For Respondents Who See Friends with Great Frequency				
Low	21%	33%	28%	40%
Medium	37	30	34	32
High	42	37	38	28
	100	100	100	100
	(38)	(67)	(64)	(96)
	$\chi^2 = 5.8957$; df = 6; .50 > p > .25.			

examines the relationship of intimacy to Machiavellianism separately for these two groups. Controlling for frequency improves the correlations somewhat. This is especially evident in the first row of the subtables. Judging from this row, the most Machiavellian are those who see their friends frequently but whose ties to them are loose. The least Machiavellian, by contrast, are found among respondents who visit with their friends only occasionally but who are linked to them by strong bonds.

TIES WITH RELATIVES

Paradoxically, the data on ties to relatives yield different results. We have a four-item index of closeness to relatives who live outside the respondent's household. Each item lists several categories of kin—for example "your children," the "brothers or sisters" of the respondent's spouse, "your parents." The respondent indicates by check-marks to which, if any, of the categories the item applies. The score for a given item depends on the number of categories checked.

In developing items for this index, we did not specify separate dimensions of the variable but relied on a global notion of closeness. One indicator has to do with the extent to which the respondent asks advice from relatives. Two refer to the exchange of material objects—one dealing with the receiving of gifts, the other with loaning and borrowing. A fourth gauges the extent to which the respondent engages in "lively discussions" with relatives.

When cross-tabulated with Machiavellianism, the index yields a small correlation. The correlation, however, is in the opposite direction from that for intimacy of friendship ties. Thus individuals with close ties to relatives tend to be more Machiavellian than individuals with loose ties (table 4.4).

TABLE 4.4
MACHIAVELLIANISM BY CLOSENESS TO RELATIVES

	Closeness to Relatives			
Machiavellianism	*Low*	*Medium-Low*	*Medium-High*	*High*
Low	42%	30%	30%	33%
Medium	33	39	38	30
High	26	32	32	38
	100	100	100	100
	(132)	(148)	(109)	(88)

$\chi^2 = 8.112$; df = 6; $.25 > p > .10$.

Before attempting to explain the discrepancy between these data and our findings concerning intimacy of friendship ties, we should examine other facets of an individual's environment.

SOLIDARITY IN THE WORK MILIEU

As part of our attempt to explore the relation of solidarity to Machiavellianism, we have developed a measure of solidarity in the work environment. The latter is an organizational variable based on the mean score of the respondents in each hotel on an index of eight items mostly having to do with perceptions of fellow employees and of the work milieu. Since the procedures for measuring organization solidarity are discussed in detail in the next chapter, we will do no more than list the components of the variable here. These are: (1) the extent to which conflict and friction are perceived in the work environment, (2) the extent to which goodwill is judged to prevail among the personnel of a hotel, and (3) the extent to which employees have, and are perceived to have, a sense of attachment and loyalty to the hotel. The first two components are roughly equivalent to the solidary-antagonistic dimension in Sorokin's theory, the third to the intensity dimension.

Our hypothesis is that an unsolidary work environment fosters Machiavellianism among employees. The data, however, are disappointing: although organizational solidarity does correlate negatively with Machiavellianism, the correlation is a small one.[36]

If, moreover, this small negative correlation reflected the influence of the work environment, individuals who had been employed in a given hotel for only a short period would not have been sufficiently exposed to the environment for their Mach scores to be greatly affected. Hence the correlation between organizational solidarity and Mach would be smaller for these employees than for longer-term employees. The data, however, show this not to be the case. The tau-beta coefficient representing the cross-tabulation of organizational solidarity with Machiavellianism is $-.13$ for respondents who have worked in their present hotel for a year or less, but only $-.06$ for respondents who have worked there for two years or longer. The correlation is actually greater for the short-term than for the long-term employees. The degree of solidarity in the work milieu, then, appears to play a negligible role, if any at all, in accounting for a person's score on the Machiavellian variable.

THE URBANISM OF THE LOCALITY OF RESIDENCE

Guided by the general concept of solidarity, we have examined the relationship of Machiavellianism to the individual's social milieu as represented by his primary ties and by the atmosphere at his place of work. As it turns out, these variables have not been very fruitful. Perhaps the solidarity concept has little relevance to this study after all!

36. In a three by-three table, which is not shown here, the percentage points difference is only five for the first row and nine for the third row.

To discard this concept, however, would be premature. The variables we have examined thus far all refer to the respondent's *current* environment. It may be that solidarity, if it does have any influence upon Machiavellianism, can operate only during an earlier stage of a person's life, before his attitudes have become set. The difficulty of exploring this possibility is that our sample consists of adults. How can we assess the attributes of the environment in which a respondent was reared twenty or thirty years ago? Fortunately this problem is not insurmountable.

An early item in the questionnaire called on the respondent to give the name of the town or locality he lived in as an adolescent. With this information, we were able to consult the decennial census closest to each respondent's fifteenth birthday to obtain the population of the locality. If the respondent lived outside the United States during this period, we obtained the population figure from a gazetteer published around the time.

The classic essay on the city by Louis Wirth stresses an absence of solidarity as among the distinguishing features of the urban way of life. He argues that the city's gigantic size inevitably fosters a social and cultural heterogeneity, an absence of personal acquaintanceship among interacting individuals, and social interaction on the basis of segmentalized roles with a corresponding impersonality, superficiality, and transitoriness of these relations. All of these factors weaken, if not destroy, the bonds of sentiment and intimacy which tie together the inhabitants of a small town into a cohesive whole.[37]

When Wirth's conceptions of urbanism are translated into Sorokin's terminology, one can readily see that they imply an absence of solidarity. The phrase *segmentalized roles*, for example, is merely a different expression for narrow extensity. *Impersonality* and *superficiality* seem to refer largely to a low intensity. The *transitoriness* of a social relationship is but another term for short duration. If, then, Wirth's arguments are sound, the size of a locality would seem to be a valid measure of solidarity, a large size indicating a relatively low level of solidarity.

In fairness to the reader, however, we must admit that Wirth's arguments have come to be widely questioned, so that the validity of size is problematic. Relying on a wealth of empirical research on ties with friends, neighbors, extended kin, and co-workers, scholars have contended that primary groups lead a vibrant existence and play an important role in the day-to-day lives of urban inhabitants. Harold L. Wilensky and Charles N. Lebeaux, for example, interpret the evidence to mean that the "alleged anonymity, depersonalization, and rootlessness of city life may be the exception rather

37. See L. Wirth, "Urbanism as a Way of Life," *American Journal of Sociology*, 44 (July 1938): 1–24.

than the rule. The typical city dweller maintains close relations with friends among either neighbors, or people in other parts of the urban area or both." In the opinion of these writers, the available data "suggest that the breakdown of primary group life and informal controls has been greatly exaggerated."[38]

On the idea that areas within a city differ in the degree to which they are urbanized, Scott Greer says: "Although highly urbanized populations are not typical of most city dwellers (they are an extreme of a continuum), those who do exist deviate widely from the stereotype of the atomistic man. They are greatly involved in the family and kinship group, and they participate intensively in friendship and cliques." If the "stereotype" is not descriptive even of the highly urbanized segments of a city, how much less so must it be of the other segments?[39]

Most recently Aida K. Tomeh has written that a major criticism of "Wirth and others of the Chicago school is that they exaggerated the degree of secularization and disorganization that supposedly typifies urban communities." Research has disclosed "strong kinship and neighborhood ties in those areas of the city where such relations were often assumed to be quite weak."[40]

The more recent views of social life in the city, then, differ sharply in emphasis from those of Wirth—if, indeed, the two sets of views are not in outright conflict with each other. The proponents of these newer views, moreover, can marshal an impressive array of empirical studies to support the contention that isolation from friends and kin is a rare occurrence in the city.[41]

Despite the formidable case that Wirth's detractors appear to have made out, it is our thesis that they have not done full justice to his conception of urban life. When one examines the studies on which their arguments are based, he discovers that—with two partial exceptions that are discussed later on[42]—these studies are less than adequate for testing Wirth's views. To begin with, the measures employed often deal with the frequency with

38. H. L. Wilensky and C. N. Lebeaux, *Industrial Society and Social Welfare* (New York: Russell Sage Foundation, 1958), pp. 122 and 125.

39. S. Greer, *The Emerging City: Myth and Reality* (New York: Free Press of Glencoe, 1962), pp. 92–93.

40. A. K. Tomeh, "Participation in a Metropolitan Community," *Sociological Quarterly*, 8 (1967):85.

41. A number of these studies are cited in notes 43 and 46 below.

42. The partial exceptions are J. P. Sutcliffe and B. D. Crabbe, "Incidence and Degrees of Friendship in Urban and Rural Areas," *Social Forces*, 42 (October 1963):60–67, and W. H. Key, "Rural-Urban Differences and the Family," *Sociological Quarterly*, 2 (1961):49–56. These studies are discussed in note 55 below.

which an individual interacts, or gets together socially, with his associates.[43] The high rate of interaction that is generally found among city dwellers is thought to refute Wirth's views. The fallacy here is that Wirth was not concerned with the *quantity* of interaction. In one passage, for example, he explicitly remarked, "This is not to say that the urban inhabitants have fewer acquaintances than rural inhabitants, for the reverse may actually be true. . . ."[44] His concern, rather, was with the *quality* of interaction or solidarity. Thus he spoke of the "impersonal, superficial, transitory, and segmental" character of social ties in the city and of "the reserve, the indifference, and the blasé outlook which urbanites manifest in their relationships."[45] Insofar as the measures used in the empirical research do not tap the dimensions implicit in Wirth's discussion, this research cannot be regarded as truly testing his ideas.

One must immediately concede that there are studies that do use indicators referring to the solidarity of social relations. But even these investigations leave something to be desired. For they are not comparative. The samples are confined to persons living in large cities, so that they do not permit one to make inferences about differences between urban areas, on the one side, and small towns and rural areas, on the other.[46] As Wirth observed in one passage: "We must . . . infer that urbanism will assume its most characteristic and extreme form in the measure in which the conditions with which it is congruent are present. Thus the larger, the more densely

43. For studies dealing with frequency of interaction with associates, see S. Greer, "Urbanism Reconsidered: A Comparative Study of Local Areas in a Metropolis," *American Sociological Review*, 21 (1956):19–24; S. Greer and E. Kube, "Urbanism and Social Structure: A Los Angeles Study," in M. B. Sussman, ed., *Community Structure and Analysis* (New York: Thomas Y. Crowell, 1959), pp. 93–112; M. Axelrod, "Urban Structure and Social Participation," *American Sociological Review*, 21 (1956):13–18; A. K. Tomeh, "Informal Group Participation and Residential Patterns," *American Journal of Sociology*, 70 (July 1964):28–35; and Tomeh, "Participation in a Metropolitan Community," pp. 85–102.

44. Wirth, "Urbanism as a Way of Life," p. 12.

45. Ibid.

46. For investigations that contain measures of the quality of social relations but are not comparative in their design, see W. Bell and M. T. Boat, "Urban Neighborhoods and Informal Social Relations," *American Journal of Sociology*, 62 (1957):391–98; M. B. Sussman, "The Isolated Nuclear Family: Fact or Fiction," *Social Forces*, 6 (1959):333–40; N. Babchuck and A. P. Bates, "The Primary Relations of Middle-Class Couples," *American Sociological Review*, 28 (June 1963):377–84; and N. Babchuck, "Primary Friends and Kin: A Study of the Associations of Middle-Class Couples," *Social Forces*, 43 (May 1965): 483–93. Two reviews of research focusing on the quality of ties among extended kin are M. B. Sussman and L. Burchinal, "Kin Family Network: Unheralded Structure in Current Conceptualizations of Family Functioning," *Marriage and Family Living*, 24 (1962): 231–40; and J. Aldous, "Urbanization, The Extended Family and Kinship Ties in West Africa," *Social Forces*, 41 (October 1962):6–11.

populated, and the more heterogeneous a community, the more accentuated the characteristics associated with urbanism will be."[47] To the extent that Wirth intended to depict the ways in which highly urbanized settlements differ from less urbanized settlements, the absence of a comparative design vitiates the existing studies as a test of his theory.[48]

Finally, these studies are limited to relations with kin, friends, neighbors, and the like. To be sure, the studies frequently touch on relations with co-workers, but such relations are invariably viewed in terms of leisure-time, friendship activities. What is wrong here is that the relationships that these studies focus on constitute only a part of any person's network of social relations. Wirth never intended to confine his analysis to that part. On the contrary, his interest was in the total network. Consider his remark that the "distinctive features of the urban mode of life have often been described sociologically as consisting of the substitution of secondary for primary contacts";[49] or his mention of the "number of people . . . with whom they [urban inhabitants] rub elbows in the course of daily life";[50] or his reference to the absence of "sentimental and emotional ties" and to "a spirit of competition, aggrandizement, and mutual exploitation."[51] The language Wirth uses in these and other passages seems to refer in large part to economic and business relationships. Because the existing studies are confined to ties with friends and kin, they fail to deal with the secondary types of interaction that play a large role in most urbanites' day-to-day existence. Thus even if research were to demonstrate that ties with friends and kin are no less "impersonal, superficial, transitory, and segmental" in the city than in small towns and rural areas, it would still not justify rejection of Wirth's ideas inasmuch as it would tell us nothing about the comparative solidarity of social relations outside of the kin and friendship networks.

Wirth's critics, then, appear to have allowed the deficiencies and limitations of the existing studies to lead them astray.[52] Instead of designing investigations that would come to grips with the subtlety and complexity of Wirth's

47. Wirth, "Urbanism as a Way of Life," p. 9.

48. Admittedly there are studies that compare residents of census tracts that vary in their degree of "urbanism" or "family status." But in a given study, these tracts are taken from a single metropolitan area. Whatever the merits of such studies, they are no substitute for research comparing residents of different sized localities. For examples of research making intrametropolitan comparisons, see Greer, "Urbanism Reconsidered"; Greer and Kuba, "Urbanism and Social Structure"; Bell and Boat, "Urban Neighborhoods"; and Tomeh, "Informal Group Participation and Residential Patterns."

49. Wirth, "Urbanism as a Way of Life," pp. 20–21.

50. Ibid., p. 12.

51. Ibid., p. 15.

52. Let us emphasize that in calling attention to the inadequacies of the studies cited here, we are speaking strictly from the standpoint of their suitability for testing Wirth's theory.

theory, they implicitly reinterpreted the theory so as to make it congruent with the procedures that the researchers had used—and in doing so, they stripped it of its trenchant qualities.

In addition to these considerations rebutting the critics, we have data which —by showing a negative correlation between the intimacy of friendship ties and the size of the locality in which a person lives—support Wirth's depiction of social relations in the city. Insofar as they lend such support, these data also provide some evidence for the validity of the size of the locality as an indicator of solidarity.

Our procedures avoid two of the pitfalls of previous investigations. For one thing, the index of intimacy employed here seems a reasonably valid measure of the solidarity of friendship relations. For another, the sample includes residents of both large cities and small towns, thus permitting comparisons of respondents in the two.

To measure the size of the locality, we have relied on an item in the questionnaire which asked the respondent to name the "town (or locality) and state" in which he was living at the time he took the questionnaire. With this information, it was easy to go to the 1960 census to obtain the population of the locale. If a respondent resided in an urbanized area, the size variable refers to the population of the urbanized area—not the population of the municipality—in which he lived. Three urbanized areas were included in the study. Two of them, Boston and Washington, had populations of between 1.5 and 2.5 millions; the third, New York City, a population of slightly over 14 million.[53] Of the respondents who lived outside of these three areas, none lived in communities having more than 120,000 inhabitants, over 90 percent lived in towns having less than 40,000 population, and over 75 percent lived in towns having less than 20,000 population.

Table 4.5 examines the relation of intimacy to the size of the locale the respondent lived in at the time of the field work. The data show a negative correlation: residents of large cities and their suburbs are less likely to have close friendships than residents of small towns. Insofar as this finding evidences the relatively unsolidary character of social relations in urban settings, it raises even further doubts about the arguments of Wirth's detractors.

From other standpoints, including that of their intrinsic merit, these investigations may be unexceptionable.

53. The urbanized area is a census concept that refers to a large city—in the 1960 census, one of 50,000 or more population—and the surrounding suburban territory. The effect of using the urbanized area instead of the town or city as the unit for measuring population is to classify suburbs by the population of the total urban complexes of which they are part. For a formal definition of the urbanized area, see U.S. Bureau of the Census, *United States Census of Population: 1960*, vol. 1, *Characteristics of Population*, part A, *Number of Inhabitants* (Washington, D.C.: Government Printing Office, 1961), pp. xviii–xix.

TABLE 4.5
INTIMACY OF FRIENDSHIP TIES BY POPULATION OF URBANIZED AREA OR LOCALITY (IF OUTSIDE U.A.) WHERE RESPONDENT CURRENTLY LIVES

	Population		
Intimacy	*Under 120 Thousand*	*Between 1.5 and 2.5 Million*	*14 Million*
Low	42%	47%	58%
Medium	24	26	19
High	34	27	23
	100	100	100
	(131)	(185)	(145)

$\chi^2 = 8.77$; df = 4; $.10 > p > .05$.

Given the limitations of our data[54] and given the discrepancies between our findings and those of two previous comparable studies,[55] it would clearly be unwarranted to argue that this discussion has confirmed Wirth's

54. Although our data are highly suggestive, they nonetheless do have certain distinct limitations. First, the sampling procedures employed make it hazardous to generalize the findings. Aside from the fact that the sample was confined to white-collar and managerial employees in the hotel industry, selection of the hotels for inclusion in the study was not based on probability sampling procedures. Added to this is the fact that in three of the hotels the proportion of the intended sample that refused to participate was exceedingly high (i.e., over 30 percent). These three hotels were all in urbanized areas of one and a half million or more inhabitants. That the high refusal rate is not evenly distributed over the range of the independent variable may have biased the findings here. (There is some evidence, though, that the effect of the high refusal rates operates against the arguments presented here. We know that the proportion of respondents who are Machiavellian is somewhat lower in the hotels with the high refusal rates than in the other hotels located in the cities of the same size. We also know that there is a slight negative correlation between an individual's Machiavellianism score and the intimacy of his friendship ties. Thus the high refusal rates may have served artificially to raise the percentage in the cities having high intimacy scores and thereby spuriously to lower the correlation between size of locale and intimacy. This is only surmise on our part. But if it is correct, the evidence offered here in support of Wirth would have been even more favorable to his position had the high refusal rates not occurred.)

A second limitation is that the only measure of the solidarity of a person's social relations used here is that of the respondent's friendship ties. We have presented data neither on relations with extended kin nor on relations with other kinds of associates. (We do have an index of closeness to relatives, but, for reasons that we explain at the end of this chapter, we do not regard this index as a valid measure of solidarity.)

Finally, the index of the intimacy of friendship ties is based solely on the respondent's report. We did not give questionnaires to the five friends named by each respondent in order to check the reliability of his report.

55. The discrepancies emerge from two studies that offer data comparable to those presented here. Sutcliffe and Crabbe studied five groups—each consisting of eight Australian first-year university students—matched on a number of variables. The first three groups lived

theory of urbanism as a way of life. Nevertheless, the arguments and the evidence presented here do suggest that the size of the locality probably has validity as an indicator of solidarity.

We argued above that, since the solidarity of the respondent's current environment did not take us very far in explaining the origins of the Machiavellian outlook, it might be worthwhile to examine the solidarity of the

---

in Sydney, the fourth in the suburbs, and the fifth in towns of less than 40,000 population. After listing all of the "various people you know and meet," the respondents answered seven items about their relationship with each such person. On the basis of the replies the persons named were classified into three categories varying in degrees of friendship—"best friend," "friend," and "acquaintance." The findings of the study unfortunately were equivocal. The respondents who lived in the small towns characterized fewer persons as "best friends" than the respondents who lived in the urban and suburban areas. If, however, one lumps the "best friends" and the "friends" together, it turns out that the findings are just the opposite: the small town residents named a greater number than the urbanites and the suburbanites. (See Sutcliffe and Crabbe, "Incidence and Degrees of Friendship.")

With a Guttman scale measuring participation in the extended family, Key studied 357 individuals who lived in different sized localities in the Midwest. He failed to find any linear relation between size and participation. His results are thus at variance with those presented here. (See Key, "Rural-Urban Differences.")

The discrepancies between these two studies and the present one can perhaps be explained by examining some differences in the research procedures. First, the studies did not measure the solidarity of social relations in the same manner. The items in the Sutcliffe and Crabbe study deal with such things as willingness to lend articles, the amount of confiding, and willingness to support the other person in the face of criticism. Aside from the fact that Key's measure refers to kin while ours refers to friends, his measure is conceptually impure in that it contains items that gauge both the frequency of interaction and solidarity. And only a minority of the five items in his scale—one dealing with the frequency of lending and borrowing and the other with the frequency of "favors other than lending" —measure solidarity. Thus the measures used in these studies seem to be tapping dimensions that are different from those on which the present study is based (intensity, extensity, duration, and interconnectedness of the social network). In our opinion, the measure used here does a much better job of capturing the nuances of solidarity as Wirth implicitly conceived it in his essay. In any event, the correlation between urbanism and the solidarity of social relations could conceivably depend on the dimensions used to measure the latter variable.

In addition, Key's study uses different cutting points for the population variable than those used here. In his data the category at the high end of this variable consists of metropolitan areas of more than 100,000 population. In this study, by contrast, the medium and high categories consist of urbanized areas having at least 1.5 million population. One doubts that most, if any, of the respondents in his high category would fall into the medium or high category in the present study. If so, the discrepancies in our findings could, in part, be due to the fact that we focused on different portions of the population variable. Should this conjecture be true, there may be a relationship between urbanism and the solidarity of social relation, but it may hold only for the upper portion of the urbanism variable. In other words, it is conceivable that disintegration in the solidarity of relations does not occur in marked form except in metropolitan areas of several million inhabitants.

respondent's environment at an earlier stage of his life—adolescence. As a measure of this property, we shall employ the population of the community in which the respondent spent most of that stage of his life. Table 4.6 gives the cross-tabulation of this variable with Machiavellianism.

TABLE 4.6

MACHIAVELLIANISM BY THE POPULATION OF THE URBANIZED AREA OR LOCALITY (IF OUTSIDE U.A.) WHERE THE RESPONDENT LIVED AS AN ADOLESCENT

	Population (in thousands)		
Machiavellianism	*Under 50*	*50–999*	*1,000 or more*
Low	39%	38%	26%
Medium	32	39	35
High	29	23	39
	100	100	100
	(177)	(110)	(180)

$\chi^2 = 5.088$; df $= 6$; $.75 > p > .50$.

In this table, a respondent who lived in an urbanized area is classified by the population of the area, and one who lived outside an urbanized area (in a small town, for example) or in a foreign country is classified by the size of the locality. The data indicate a positive correlation between population and Machiavellianism. The greater the urbanization of the community the respondent lived in during his teens, the more likely he is to be Machiavellian.

The correlation, however, is spuriously low. In three of the hotels in which we administered questionnaires, more than 30 percent of the prospective respondents refused to participate in the study—an unfortunate occurrence the circumstances of which have already been explained in the first chapter. One consequence is that the proportion of respondents who are Machiavellian is somewhat lower in these hotels than in the other hotels located in cities of the same size. The three hotels are all in cities of one million or more inhabitants. Since there is a correlation between the size of the community the respondent currently works in and the size of the community he spent his adolescence in, the result is artificially to reduce the number of Machiavellians who lived in highly urbanized environments and thus lower the correlation between adolescent population and Machiavellianism.

We have therefore divided the sample in two and run the cross-tabulation separately for respondents from hotels with high refusal rates and respondents from hotels with low refusal rates. Controlling for the refusal rate in this way improves the percentage differences, especially in the case of hotels with low refusal rates.[56]

56. This three-variable table is not given in the text.

Another factor making the correlation spuriously low is the inclusion in the above tables of respondents who lived in foreign countries during adolescence. Since we obtained population figures for these respondents from gazetteers and not from the census, we have only the population of the town or city in which the respondent lived. If his locality was part of a larger urban area, we were unable to code the population of the latter.

Table 4.7 excludes respondents who spent their adolescence outside the United States. It is based, moreover, only on employees in hotels with low refusal rates since some of the column N's in the corresponding table for hotels with high refusal rates are too small for the table to be meaningful.

The correlation in table 4.7 is substantial. Not only does the immediate milieu of the family affect Machiavellianism, as we saw in an earlier chapter; the larger environment of the area in which an adolescent lives, does so as well.

TABLE 4.7
MACHIAVELLIANISM BY THE POPULATION OF THE URBANIZED AREA OR LOCALITY (IF OUTSIDE U.A.) WHERE THE RESPONDENT LIVED AS AN ADOLESCENT

	Population (in thousands)		
Machiavellianism	*Under 50*	*50–999*	*1,000 or more*
Low	37%	33%	24%
Medium	36	37	27
High	27	30	49
	100	100	100
	(128)	(57)	(75)

$\chi^2 = 10.949$; df = 4; $.05 > p > .025$.

NOTE: Only respondents from low-refusal hotels who spent their adolescence in the U.S. are included.

Can we say anything further about the operation of solidarity during adolescence? Data which we have not presented here indicate that when suburbs are classified by their own population—and not by the population of the urbanized areas in which they are included—there is practically no correlation between Machiavellianism and the size of the locality the respondent lived in as an adolescent. It is only when we group suburbs with cities that a correlation between population and Machiavellianism shows up—a fact which suggests that spending one's youth in a suburb instead of in the center of an urban complex does not result in a lower Mach score.

This inference is corroborated by the empirical evidence. Despite the greater physical resemblance that suburban neighborhoods—with their lower population densities and their one-unit dwellings—have to small towns than to large cities, a suburban adolescence is not associated with a lower Mach score than an urban adolescence. Indeed, a slightly higher proportion of the suburban youth turn out to be Machiavellian.[57]

A similar finding emerges when we use one of the items in the questionnaire to measure "suburbanism." This item required the respondent to characterize the physical complexion of the block he resided on between the ages of twelve and eighteen. He could check one of several possible replies ranging from "all apartment buildings" to "all houses." When the item is cross-tabulated with Machiavellianism for respondents who lived in urbanized areas or cities of at least a million inhabitants, it turns out that the Machiavellians come from the suburban-type neighborhoods in greater frequency than they come from the urban-type neighborhoods.[58]

The last two findings suggest that the correlation between urban residence during adolescence (as measured by population) and Machiavellianism is not due to the milieu of the immediate neighborhood. Living in a central city (as opposed to living in the suburbs) or living on a block of apartment buildings (as opposed to living on a block of houses) does not result in greater Machiavellianism. Since it is not the immediate neighborhood that accounts for the correlation between urbanism and Mach, it must be something about the environment of the larger area that does. Unfortunately the data do not permit further exploration of what this something is.

TABLE 4.8
MACHIAVELLIANISM BY POPULATION OF URBANIZED AREA OR LOCALITY (IF OUTSIDE U.A.) WHERE RESPONDENT CURRENTLY LIVES

	Population		
Machiavellianism	*Under 120 Thousand*	*1.5–2.5 Million*	*14 Million*
Low	34%	34%	35%
Medium	36	32	37
High	30	35	28
	100	100	100
	(133)	(197)	(150)

$\chi^2 = 1.852$; df = 4; $.90 > p > .75$.

57. In the relevant table, which is not presented here, whether the respondent resided in an urban center or in the suburbs was ascertained directly from the census. He was classified as living in an urban center if he lived in an urbanized area and his locality had a population of 50,000 or more. His locality was defined as a suburb if it was situated in an urbanized area but had a population of less than 50,000. These were the criteria for distinguishing between suburbs and urban areas in the census from 1930 to 1960. In earlier censuses slightly different criteria were used.

58. Space limitations prohibit presentation of this cross-tabulation.

If Machiavellianism correlates with the population of the area the respondent lived in as a youth, does it also correlate with the population of the locality in which he currently resides? The data indicate that it does not (table 4.8). Controlling for the rate of refusals in the hotel in which the respondent is employed, fails to produce a correlation.[59]

Thus the degree of urbanism of a person's residence as an adult has little or no effect on his Machiavellian score. This is brought out vividly by running the population of the adolescent residence and that of the current residence simultaneously against Machiavellianism (table 4.9). Reading across the rows, we see that the size of the home area during adolescence and Machiavellianism still correlate. But comparing the first and second rows of each column discloses that there is no consistent relationship between the population of the area currently lived in and Machiavellianism. These data confirm an implication of the previous discussion: whatever accounts for the effects of urbanism, it evidently operates only during the formative years of adolescence.

TABLE 4.9

PERCENT HIGH ON MACHIAVELLIANISM BY POPULATION OF URBANIZED AREA OR LOCALITY (IF OUTSIDE U.A.) WHERE RESPONDENT LIVED DURING ADOLESCENCE AND WHERE HE CURRENTLY LIVES

	Adolescent Population (in thousands)		
Current Population	*Under 50*	*50–999*	*1,000 or more*
Under 120 thousand	27% (82)	26% (27)	45% (20)
1.5 million or more	33% (58)	23% (47)	52% (56)

A vs. B vs. C: $\chi^2 = 2.65$; df = 2; .50 > p > .25. D vs. E vs. F: $\chi^2 = 9.20$; df = 2; .025 > p > .01. A vs. D: $\chi^2 = .28$; df = 1; .75 > p > .50. B vs. E: $\chi^2 = 0$. C vs. F: $\chi^2 = .08$; df = 1; .50 > p > .25.

NOTE: Only respondents from hotels with low refusal rates are included. (There is no corresponding table for the hotels with high refusal rates since almost all of the respondents in these hotels live in areas with populations of one and a half million or more.)

Our understanding of the urbanism variable is further enhanced when we consider it in conjunction with the variables pertaining to the respondent's recollection of his parents. We will deal with the latter by using the composite index of parent variables. This index, the reader will recall, simply aggregates each respondent's scores on our four parental variables. A high score on the composite index indicates that the family milieu of a respondent, as he was growing up, conduced to Machiavellian attitudes.

59. The tables controlling for the refusal rate are not shown here.

We have already pointed out the reasons for running separate tables for hotels with low refusal rates and those with high refusal rates when analyzing the urbanism variable. The present discussion will be concerned only with respondents from hotels with low refusal rates. This is necessary for several reasons. One is that the sample in hotels with high refusal rates is too small to permit the simultaneous cross-tabulation of more than two variables. Almost a third of the respondents in these hotels, moreover, spent their adolescence in countries outside the United States. It would therefore be necessary to control for the country of residence since, lacking census data for these countries, we were not able properly to classify foreign suburban communities on the urbanism variable.

The cross-tabulation procedure can be unwieldy when the purpose is to point up how the correlation between two variables varies under different conditions. This is especially so when one or more of the variables in the analysis has more than two categories. The presentation will therefore make use of the tau-beta correlation coefficient when appropriate.[60]

Table 4.10 presents the tau-beta coefficients for the correlation between the urbanism of the adolescent residence and Machiavellianism for different scores on the composite index of parent variables. As the reader can see, the coefficients progressively increase in magnitude with each category of the parent index.

TABLE 4.10
CORRELATION BETWEEN POPULATION OF URBANIZED AREA OR LOCALITY (IF OUTSIDE U.A.) AND MACHIAVELLIANISM BY SCORE ON COMPOSITE INDEX OF PARENT VARIABLES

Parent Index	*Tau-Beta Coefficient*	
Low	−.06	(55)
Medium-Low	.09	(79)
Medium-High	.14	(69)
High	.32	(46)

NOTE: Only respondents from hotels with low refusal rates are included.

We can perhaps illuminate the above coefficients by presenting the subtables for the low category and the high category of the parent variable (table 4.11). (To simplify the presentation, we omit the subtables for the

60. The tau-beta coefficient is a measure of rank correlation. The cross-tabulation program of the Bureau of Applied Social Research at Columbia University has an option for stating the coefficient associated with a given table or subtable. See instructions for "CROSSTAB-MPCRTB," mimeographed, (Bureau of Applied Social Research, Columbia University, February 25, 1965) pp. 15–19.

two medium categories.) Of primary interest here is the third column of each table reporting the percentage points difference. By comparing the figures in this column for the two subtables, we obtain some idea of how much higher the correlation between urbanism and Machiavellianism is in the second than in the first subtable. In the first row, the difference increases from −9 points to +11 points. In the third row, the difference increases from +2 to −34 points.

TABLE 4.11

MACHIAVELLIANISM BY THE POPULATION OF THE URBANIZED AREA OR LOCALITY (IF OUTSIDE U.A.) WHERE RESPONDENT LIVED DURING ADOLESCENCE

	Adolescent Population		
Machiavellianism	*Under Million*	*Million or more*	*% Points Difference*
For Respondents Scoring Low in the Composite Index of Parent Variables			
Low	35%	44%	−9
Medium	41	33	8
High	24	22	2
	100	100	
	(46)	(9)	
	$\chi^2 = .3185$; df = 2; $.90 > p > .75$.		
For Respondents Scoring High on the Composite Index of Parent Variables			
Low	17%	6%	11
Medium	35	12	23
High	48	82	−34
	100	100	
	(29)	(17)	
	$\chi^2 = 5.1301$; df = 2; $.10 > p > .05$.		

The data suggest that if home conditions lay the groundwork for high ethical standards, the larger setting outside the family has little, if any, power to alter a person's moral outlook. Persons, on the other hand, who have been raised in family milieus that are defective in fostering the develop ment of conscience, are more subject to the influence of the larger social environment.

These data can be viewed from a different perspective by asking if the home plays the same role in communities varying in the degree of urbanization. Again, the tau-beta coefficients convey at a glance the difference between highly urbanized and less urbanized communities (table 4.12). In small-town settings the family plays a relatively minor role in determining a person's Machiavellianism. It is much more influential in the urbanized areas.

TABLE 4.12

CORRELATIONS BETWEEN MACHIAVELLIANISM AND COMPOSITE INDEX OF PARENT VARIABLES BY POPULATION OF THE URBANIZED AREA OR LOCALITY (IF OUTSIDE U.A.) WHERE RESPONDENT LIVED DURING ADOLESCENCE

Population (in thousands)	*Tau-Beta Coefficients*	
Under 50	.10	(130)
50 to 999	.16	(60)
1,000 and Over	.37	(59)

NOTE: Only respondents from hotels with low refusal rates are included.

This can also be seen by cross-tabulating a dichotomous version of the parent index with Machiavellianism separately for places of under one million inhabitants and for those of one million or more inhabitants. The major point of interest in table 4.13 is the improvement in the percentage points difference from the first subtable to the second subtable. In the first row, the change is from 8 points to 32 points; in the third row, from 14 points to 23 points.

TABLE 4.13

MACHIAVELLIANISM BY COMPOSITE INDEX OF PARENT VARIABLES

Machiavellianism	*Parent Index* Low	*Parent Index* High	*% Points Difference*
For Respondents Who Lived in Urbanized Areas or Localities (if outside U.A.) of Under One Million Population			
Low	39%	31%	8
Medium	39	33	6
High	22	36	−14
	100	100	
	(109)	(81)	
	$\chi^2 = 4.4632$; df = 2; .25 > p > .10.		
For Respondents Who Lived in Urbanized Areas or Localities (if outside U.A.) of One Million or More Population			
Low	44%	12%	32
Medium	20	29	−9
High	36	59	−23
	100	100	
	(25)	(34)	
	$\chi^2 = 7.910$; df = 2; .025 > p > .01.		

NOTE: Only respondents from hotels with low refusal rates are included.

What do our findings mean? The social atmosphere of the small town apparently makes up for many deficiences in family milieus, so that even if the home is not conducive to conventional moral development, the larger environment nevertheless tends to foster a socially acceptable moral outlook. In the highly urbanized areas, the larger environment outside the family seems deleterious to the development of conscience. Therefore the home milieu must be "wholesome" for sound ethical attitudes to take root.

These findings disclose an interesting interaction between the larger social setting and the more immediate milieu of the family and thus link the sociological perspectives derived from Toennies and Sorokin with the psychological perspective of Freud.

But perhaps these relationships are unique to the present sample. Fortunately we are in possession of some parallel data from de Miguel's study of Spanish students. Two of the items in his questionnaire, as we mentioned earlier, resemble the items of the index of rapport with parents. The correlation between each of these items and Machiavellianism was greater in the industrial provinces than in the nonindustrial provinces. Also, the relation between industrialization and Machiavellianism tended to be greater for respondents whose replies intimated low rapport with their parents than for respondents whose replies intimated high rapport.[61] This research suggests that our findings are not a fortuitous result of the particular sample used in the present study.

Interpreting the Findings

The data present several paradoxes. The urbanism of one's residential locality during adolescence correlates with Machiavellianism, but the same variable for the current period does not. The intimacy of friendship ties relates to Mach in the expected direction, but the index of closeness to kin relates in just the opposite direction. A person spends a major portion of his life working. Therefore if solidarity is a sound explanatory concept, one would expect the organizational solidarity variable to correlate significantly with Machiavellianism. Yet it does not. Is there any explanation for these discrepancies? Can we make sense of them?

We have seen that, taken together, variables referring to the preadult period—that is, variables concerning the parents and the urbanism of the home community—show a strong correlation with Machiavellianism. The early time reference suggests that these are causal factors. Moreover, these variables represent elements of the environment over which the respondent had little control. He could not, for example, decide the population

61. See de Miguel, "Social Correlates of Machiavellianism," pp. 21–23.

of the community in which his family lived. This, too, indicates that the preadult variables are to be considered independent variables.

If a variable that acts as a causal factor at one stage does not show a correlation with the dependent variable at another stage, one can infer that the formative influences can occur only during the first stage. So if the population of the respondent's present place of living does not correlate with Machiavellianism, it is probably because he is past the stage of his life where such a variable can have an influence. Most likely Machiavellianism is a relatively stable characteristic molded by influences during childhood and adolescence and usually not subject to much change after a person enters adulthood. This would also explain why the solidarity of the work organization shows a negligible relationship to Machiavellianism.

If this line of reasoning is correct, what are we to make of the association between Machiavellianism and intimacy of friendship? We suspect, although we cannot demonstrate it, that intimacy does not really operate as a causal factor but as a dependent variable. The character of a person's friendship ties fundamentally differs from variables such as urbanism and organizational solidarity in that it is more likely to reflect his personal predispositions. According to this interpretation, Machiavellians have less capacity than non-Machiavellians for close friendships. The intervening process hypothesized here is the weak strength of emotional attachments that we suspect Machiavellians have. Being uninclined to invest strong emotions in his ties with others, the Machiavellian has a smaller propensity for intimacy with friends.

Assuming that this conjecture is correct, we still have not explained the positive association of Machiavellianism with closeness to relatives. If Machiavellians invest less affect in their social relations, their ties to kin should be more distant, not less distant, as we have found. The key to this puzzle, we surmise, lies in our measurement of the closeness variable. Before devising an index of intimacy with friends, we were careful to delineate the component dimensions. These dimensions were based on a a body of theory that had been developed by classical sociologists culminating in Sorokin's modalities of the social system of interaction. It was on the basis of these theoretically grounded dimensions that we formulated the items for the index. This was not the case with the index of closeness to relatives. Here item formulation was guided by a more global, intuitive notion of what constitutes closeness. So the items are based on a common-sense notion of closeness, not on theoretically derived dimensions. This, in our judgment, is a fatal flaw in the index. The closeness of primary relations represents a conceptually complex variable. Unless measurement is based on sound conceptualization, it will be of doubtful validity.

We have some evidence for this point. One of the items that we originally included in the series about friendship ties but that we left out of the index of intimacy strongly resembles, in its wording, an item in the index of closeness to relatives. It reads, "You have asked this person for advice about a personal matter within the last six months." When cross-tabulated with Machiavellianism, this item yields a positive, not a negative, correlation.[62] This is revealing since the association between the intimacy of friendship ties and Machiavellianism is negative. We can infer that not just any item conforming to our common-sense notion of closeness is valid if by closeness we mean the dimensions employed in a theoretical system such as that of Sorokin. The failure, then, of closeness to relatives to correlate negatively with Machiavellianism reflects, if the argument here is correct, a failure to specify the dimensions of the closeness variable.

Conclusions

Part I of this study has employed the theories of Freud, Cooley, and Toennies primarily for heuristic purposes. Our interest has been in the variables that these theories suggest be examined in order to study the origins of Machiavellianism. Since the findings are largely consistent with all three theories, there is a need for a theoretical synthesis that will order the data.

If we have made a contribution in this study, however, it has not been to suggest a synthesis. It has been, rather, to show that the parental variables that the psychologists have been focusing on in their studies of conscience do not operate in the same manner in all social environments. There is an interaction—in the statistical sense—between parental behavior and social environment. The developmental psychologists are in a much better position than we are to effect a theoretical synthesis. But any such synthesis will have to account for the interaction effect. Insofar as any theory of conscience ignores the larger environment outside the family, it must be regarded as incomplete.

62. This cross-tabulation is not presented here.

PART II

SOLIDARITY IN THE WORK ENVIRONMENT

CHAPTER 5

Some Preliminary Considerations

WE INITIALLY conceived of solidarity as a set of factors acting as independent variables in relation to Machiavellianism. As we saw earlier, however, the data did not bear out this approach with respect to the solidarity of the work environment. After the analysis of the data was well under way, these disappointing results led to a new area of study, an area which we had not anticipated when we originally planned the research design. If solidarity in the work milieu does not operate as an independent variable, we asked ourselves, why not view it as a dependent variable? Why not explore the factors which make for more or less solidarity?

The research reported in Part II concentrates on these questions. As such, it discards Machiavellianism as the center of the study—although not entirely. For this index enters as a constituent into those factors which account for variations in solidarity.

The Indices of Solidarity at Work

The analysis is conducted on two levels. On the one hand, we engage in contextual analysis, in which most of the independent variables are characteristics of the hotel environment, that is to say, properties of collectivities. These are used to account for the perceptions and feelings respondents have about other employees and about the social milieu at work. Hence the dependent variable in the contextual analysis refers to the characteristics of individuals.[1] On the second level of analysis, both independent variables and

1. Among the methodological discussions of contextual analysis are P. F. Lazarsfeld and H. Menzel, "On the Relation Between Individual and Collective Properties," in A. Etzioni, ed., *Complex Organizations* (New York: Holt, Rinehart and Winston, 1961), pp. 422–40; P. M. Blau, "Formal Organizations: Dimensions of Analysis," *American Journal of Sociology*, 63 (1957):58–69; P. M. Blau, "Structural Effects," *American Sociological Review*, 25 (1960):178–93; J. A. Davis et al., "A Technique for Analyzing the Effects of Group Composition," *American Sociological Review*, 26 (1961):215–25; and A. S. Tannenbaum and J. G. Bachman, "Structural Versus Individual Effects," *American Journal of Sociology*, 69 (1964):585–95.

dependent variables refer to collectivities. Here we aggregate the perceptions and attitudes of respondents in each hotel to arrive at a measure of solidarity for that hotel. The units of analysis are not individual respondents, as in contextual analysis, but hotels.

The contextual analysis centers on an index of solidary feelings, or, as we shall often refer to it, the SF index. This measure, which consists of eight items, can be divided roughly into three components. The first pertains to the respondent's perceptions of conflict and friction in his work milieu. The questionnaire, for example, inquires "how many separate disputes or quarrels have you heard of or personally witnessed . . . between managerial and non-managerial employees" within the preceding three weeks? A second set of items measures the respondent's judgment of the extent to which good will prevails among the personnel of a hotel. These items ask the respondent how "considerate" employees are of each other and whether they "distrust each other." The final component has to do with the degree of attachment or allegiance the respondent thinks other employees have to the hotel and with the degree which he himself has to the hotel. One item reads, "Judging from the people with whom you have contact, how much loyalty to the hotel is there" among nonexecutive personnel? Thus the SF index refers, in its face content, primarily to the degree of harmony and cooperation that the respondent perceives in his work milieu.[2]

The judgmental character of most of the items derives from the purpose for which the index was originally intended. Our original intention, it will be recalled, was to use solidarity as a property of the organizational environment, examining through contextual analysis the effects it has on the Machiavellianism of individuals. In such an analysis, the accurate measurement of each individual's own attitudes and behavior is unnecessary. If we are going to aggregate the responses of individual respondents to form a collective measure, perceptual data will suffice. Indeed, such data have a certain advantage. Items about such things as interpersonal conflict and loyalty to one's employer are marred by social desirability. When we ask about a person's own behavior or attitudes, we are likely to elicit from many respondents not expressions of true feeling, but replies that they regard as socially acceptable. This especially holds when the research is being conducted in an industrial setting, where many respondents are distrustful and skeptical toward a study despite the assurances of confidentiality the investigator may give. It was, for these reasons, felt that the solidarity items

2. Only one item in the index is nonperceptual. Intended to tap the respondent's over-all attachment to the hotel, it asks how he would feel if "circumstances compelled you to leave your job . . . and take *similar work* with *similar pay* elsewhere."

would serve their function better if they asked about other people instead of about the respondent himself.

Once we think of solidarity as a dependent variable, however, the items of the SF index take on a different function, and it is open to question whether, as presently worded, they are suited for an index designed to measure the characteristics of individuals. On an individual level, we are not so much interested in a person's perceptions of others as we are in how he himself acts in the work milieu and how he himself feels toward his job and toward his place of work. Whether he feels other employees trust or distrust each other, for example, is of less interest than the extent to which he himself trusts or distrusts other personnel in the hotel. So the predominantly perceptual character of the SF index seems, at first thought, to vitiate its use as a measure of individual characteristics.

We believe, however, that this is in fact not the case. The SF index, to be sure, refers primarily to perceptions of the environment, and, from a strictly logical point of view, one can, from a person's response to a perceptual item, make inferences only about his perceptions. If a person says that his fellow employees distrust each other, one cannot logically infer that he himself is a distrustful individual. Nevertheless, it would be fallacious to contend that an index measures only what is deducible, in a strict logical fashion, from the face content of the items comprising the index.

We can perhaps clarify this point by referring to the distinction that P. F. Lazarsfeld makes between expressive and predictive indicators.[3] One can think of the indicators of a concept, he argues, as forming layers in a causal chain, some of which will be close to the "originating observation." The latter is, in a sense, a dependent variable, variations in which the concept is meant to explain. Other indicators will be closer to the concept itself. Indicators referring to the originating observation are labeled predictive indicators, while those tied more closely to the concept Lazarsfeld calls expressive indicators. To illustrate this distinction, he applies it to the authoritarian personality. There could be several possible types of predictive indicators since the authoritarian personality is meant to explain more than one dependent variable. Predictive indicators might, for example, refer to anti-Semitic attitudes or to the likelihood of a person resisting the rise of fascism. By contrast, expressive indicators would be those referring directly to those personality tendencies, such as "weakness of the ego" or "intolerance of ambiguity," thought to underlie the originating observations. The essential point, for our purposes, is that the indicators of a variable

3. See P. F. Lazarsfeld, "Problems in Methodology," in R. K. Merton et al., eds., *Sociology Today: Problems and Prospects* (New York: Basic Books, 1959), pp. 47–60.

need not be directly related, in terms of their face content, to that variable. They may be one or more steps removed from the variable of interest.

In light of Lazarsfeld's discussion, we think it reasonable to argue that, although the SF index refers primarily to the respondent's perceptions of his work milieu, it indirectly measures his satisfaction with that milieu. Its component items, in other words, are principally indicators that lie closer to the expressive than to the predictive end of the expressive-predictive continuum. If a respondent says that employees have little loyalty to the hotel, that they are lacking in consideration for one another, that they quarrel often, that the relationship between the management and the rank and file is a hostile one—the picture he is presenting is hardly one that suggests high morale and fiery enthusiasm for his place of work. Conversely, if a respondent depicts his fellow employees as devoted to their employer, as working together harmoniously, as having friendly relations with the management, as trusting each other—he appears to be implicitly saying that he is satisfied, if not contented, with the hotel where he works. The SF index, then, appears to have meaning on the individual level in that it consists predominantly of expressive indicators which indirectly tell us about the level of morale and work satisfaction of a respondent.

In the absence of direct predictive indicators of these things, it seems scientifically acceptable to use the index as a substitute for such measures. Indeed, since the SF index has yielded some fruitful results, it would be a scientific waste not to report the findings. For reporting them at least leaves open the possibility that future investigators will replicate the findings with better indices. If, however, we were to withhold the findings, such replication would be ruled out.

Our confidence in the validity of the SF index as a measure of morale is enhanced when we examine the correlation of the perceptual items with the one nonperceptual item. This item, inquiring how the respondent would feel about having to leave his job at the hotel, appears to get at his satisfaction with the work milieu and is thus an indicator of morale as the word is commonly understood. If all the other items from the SF index correlate with this one item, such correlations constitute some evidence—admittedly not conclusive—that the index does, in fact, measure morale. The tau-beta coefficients for the relevant cross-tabulations vary between .10 and .33. The median coefficient is .19. These correlations, which for the most part are fairly substantial in magnitude, are consistent with our contention as to what the SF index measures.[4]

4. Further evidence for the validity of the SF index comes from a study showing that conflict among different units of an organization is inversely correlated with the morale of the members in several kinds of organizations. See C. G. Smith, "A Comparative Analysis of

In addition to measuring individual attitudes and perceptions, we wish to be able to talk about the actual state of social relations in a hotel. The SF index tells us how individuals perceive their social environment, and insofar as these perceptions are accurate, it also tells us indirectly about the environment itself. But we know that the perceptions people have of the social milieu around them are subject to distortion and to variation from one individual to the next, that these perceptions are, to some extent, a function of predispositional factors and of nuances in the environment. (In fact, we shall present data demonstrating this point in chapter 8.) It is for this reason (as well as others) that correlations found in contextual analysis do not necessarily parallel correlations found when the units of study are organizations. A variable that correlates with solidary feelings may not show an equivalent relationship to a collective measure of solidarity.

Accordingly, we have devised a measure of organizational solidarity by calculating the mean of the SF scores for the respondents in each hotel. The assumption here is that, although this measure is ultimately based on the perceptions of individuals, aggregating these perceptions minimizes the distortions and biases that are to be found in perceptual data. Hence the organizational solidarity variable is intended to measure actual variations among the hotels in those phenomena that make up solidarity—phenomena such as the prevalence of conflict among employees, the loyalty of personnel to their employer, and the good will that employees have toward one another.

In analyzing the data on organizational solidarity, we have departed from the cross-tabulation procedure used in the other parts of the study. This is unavoidable inasmuch as the units of analysis, hotels, are too few to permit meaningful tables embodying cross-tabulations. In lieu of such tables, we have generally employed Spearman rank-correlation coefficients.

We would prefer to devote greater attention to solidarity than to feelings of solidarity. This, however, is not feasible. Given the limited number of organizational units in the study, the analysis of more than two variables at a time is not possible when organizations are the units of analysis. Moreover, cross-tabulation tables convey the findings in a more vivid fashion than rank-correlation coefficients can and therefore are more valuable for purposes of presentation. Hence the data are presented in two forms: contextual tables with the SF index as the dependent variable and, when appropriate, Spearman coefficients representing the corresponding relationships with organizational solidarity.

Some Conditions and Consequences of Intra-Organizational Conflict," *Administrative Science Quarterly*, 10 (1966): table 4, p. 518. (Morale, in this table, is measured by the variable "identification.")

A Preview of the Analysis

Our exposition can be divided roughly into three parts. The first is primarily concerned with the personality composition of a hotel's employees. The data deal with variables such as the average Machiavellianism of a hotel's personnel and the extent of variability among the members of a unit on the Mach variable. After that, we turn our attention to the influence of certain personality characteristics of management upon solidarity in a hotel. We are not content, however, to examine these characteristics in isolation from other environmental variables. For a given characteristic of management does not operate in the same manner under all circumstances; its effects are contingent on other properties of the environment. Finally, the analysis centers on the influence of certain personality characteristics of each respondent upon his own level of solidary feelings. But we go further than correlating the properties of individuals with other properties of the same individuals inasmuch as we also seek to demonstrate that whether such correlations exist or not depends on the social context.

The Sample for This Analysis

The sample for the study as a whole is drawn from twenty-six hotels. Several considerations, however, necessitate confining this portion of the analysis to twenty-one units. For one thing, a high proportion—more than 30 percent—of the intended sample in three of the hotels refused to participate in the study. We have already cited evidence suggesting that this tended artificially to reduce the number of Machiavellians in the sample from these hotels.[5] It is also likely that the high refusal rate affected the degree of variability on the Mach scale within each of these hotels. Since we employ both variability and the average Mach score as collective variables in the present analysis, exclusion of these hotels seems justified. In one of the other hotels, we were compelled to cut short the field work just as it was getting under way, with the result that this hotel is represented in the investigation by only two respondents, both of them clerical personnel. This hotel has also been excluded.

Four of the excluded hotels are large-scale operations—that is to say, each employs more than 200 individuals and each is represented in the study by more than 25 respondents. There are several reasons for excluding such hotels. One has to do with the fact that the findings are presented primarily in the form of contextual tables. Each of the large hotels is represented by many more respondents than each of the small hotels, the smallest

5. See p. 71.

number of respondents from one of the former being 34 and the largest number being 90. By contrast, the largest number of respondents from any single unit among the small hotels is only 23. Thus the large hotels would have unduly affected the findings yielded by contextual tables had they been included in the analysis.

In addition, a number of the variables, as operationally defined in this part of the study, are not applicable to large hotels. This is so because social relations among white-collar employees in a large hotel are structured in a fundamentally different manner from such relations in a small hotel. A desk clerk in a large unit, for example, usually does not have as much contact with the general manager as one in a small unit. Also, there are more links in the chain of command between him and the general manager, so that the latter has little occasion, if any, to exercise direct supervision over him.

Or consider the interaction of people carrying out complementary functions in a hotel operation. Because of the relatively refined division of labor to be found in a large hotel, the personnel are organized into distinct departments. Most employees interact more with personnel in their own departments than with personnel in other departments, and whatever interdepartmental contacts any employee may have tend to be restricted to a certain set of individuals. The headwaiter in the elegant dining area of a large hotel, for instance, may deal with a few individuals in the accounting department, such as the food checker and the restaurant cashier, but he has little or no contact with any of the other members of that department. By contrast, the head hostess in a small unit deals with the whole accounting "department" inasmuch as the latter consists of only one or two individuals.

There are, in a sense, two populations represented in this study—one consisting of employees in large-scale hotels, the other of employees in small hotels. The pattern of social relationships is by no means the same in the two populations. Because, however, the manner in which some of our key variables operate depends on this pattern, correlations that hold for small hotels need not—and probably do not—hold for the large ones. This is an additional consideration that has prompted us to confine the analysis to the former.

CHAPTER 6

The Characteristics of the Work Environment

Interaction in the Work Milieu

IN THE course of a work day there is a fairly high rate of interaction among the types of personnel included in the sample. Whenever a hotel has two or more persons in a particular job category, they will naturally have much to do with each other. Front office clerks, for example, who work on different shifts will see each other as one is getting off work and the other coming on. The general manager and the assistant general manager will work closely together in exercising their managerial functions. The dining room manager will supervise his assistant and the hostesses.

There is perhaps even more contact among employees performing different kinds of work. The top executives have to oversee all the other personnel in the hotel.[1] Switchboard operators have to inform the desk clerks about telephone calls made by the guests so that charges for these calls can be posted in the appropriate accounts. Since all financial transactions are recorded by the accounting department, personnel who requisition supplies (for example, the chef and the head bartender) have to submit receipts to the bookkeepers. The bookkeepers also keep track of all revenue, so that desk clerks and dining room hostesses turn over cash register slips and funds on hand to them. The chefs, of course, work with the dining room personnel in planning menus, setting food prices, seeing that the dining room and the kitchen are properly coordinated, and so forth.

Aside from the intermeshing of functions, another factor fostering interaction is the physical proximity of the areas in which most of the respondents work. The front desk, the switchboard, the general manager's office, the accounting office, and secretary's desk are generally located within a few yards of each other. The kitchen and the dining room are adjacent to each other, and both are usually on the same floor as the preceding work areas. As a result, the personnel concerned cannot help seeing each other every day.

1. The phrase "top management" refers to the general manager as well as to the second-ranking executive in a hotel if the latter shares in responsibility for the over-all management of the hotel.

Given the high rate of interaction among white-collar and managerial personnel, it is reasonable to expect that the pattern of attitudes and personality traits characterizing these employees will affect the degree of solidary feelings existing in a hotel. But where should we begin in exploring such patterns? Small group studies indicating that the modal personality characteristics of members can affect the functioning of a group, provide one clue.[2] They suggest that examining the average extent of Machiavellianism prevailing among the respondents of a hotel might provide a toe hold into this area.

The Level of Machiavellianism

In order to gauge this variable, we have developed an index called the Machiavellian level of a hotel. This measure is simply the mean Mach score of all respondents from each hotel.

Cross-tabulating this variable with the SF index yields a slight inverse correlation.[3] Respondents from hotels with low Machiavellian levels are somewhat higher on SF than respondents from hotels with high Machiavellian levels. It is questionable, however, whether a genuine correlation exists, for not only is the statistical association small but there is also the possibility of spuriousness. As we shall demonstrate in chapter 8, the SF index has a fairly strong correlation with Machiavellianism when the latter is considered as an individual attribute. This raises the possibility that the Mach level correlates with solidary feelings only because the former is derived by aggregating individual Mach scores. Before we can proceed, we should test for spuriousness. Table 6.1 does this by cross-tabulating the Machiavellian level and individual Mach scores simultaneously with SF.

Among high Machiavellians, the relationship between Mach level and SF is greatly weakened. But this does not indicate spuriousness, for among the low Machiavellians, the relationship has become more marked. The findings thus signify that, although the relationship between Machiavellian level and SF depends on the Machiavellianism of the individual, there is nevertheless a definite relationship. The effects of the collective variable is confirmed on the organizational level, where we find a Spearman rank-correlation of −.27 between Mach level and organizational solidarity.

How are we to account for these findings? There are several possible

2. See, for example, W. Haythorn, "The Influence of Individual Members on the Characteristics of Small Groups," *Journal of Abnormal and Social Psychology*, 48 (1953): 276–84; R. B. Cattell et al., "The Dimensions of Syntality in Small Groups: I. The Neonate Group," *Human Relations*, 6 (1953):331–56; and N. T. Fouriezos, M. L. Hutt, and H. Guetzkow, "Measurement of Self-Oriented Needs in Discussion Groups," *Journal of Abnormal and Social Psychology*, 45 (1950):682–90.

3. The table is not shown here.

TABLE 6.1
THE PERCENTAGE HIGH ON SF BY MACHIAVELLIAN LEVEL OF HOTEL AND BY MACHIAVELLIANISM (AS AN INDIVIDUAL CHARACTERISTIC)

	Machiavellian Level	
Machiavellianism	*Low*	*High*
Low	52% (54)	28% (39)
High	31% (35)	27% (70)

A vs. B: $\chi^2 = 3.65$; df = 1; $.10 > p > .05$. C vs. D: $\chi^2 = .06$; df = 1; $.50 > p > .25$. A vs. C: $\chi^2 = 2.3$; df = 1; $.25 > p > .10$. B vs. D: $\chi^2 = .94$; df = 1; $.90 > p > .75$.

explanations. The Mach variable, as we have seen, deals in large part with the person's general attitudes toward conventional moral norms: the Machiavellian places little value on such traditional virtues as honesty, veracity, good faith, straightforwardness. What happens when the majority of people in an organization share this orientation; what are the implications for the manner in which people relate to each other? The content of the solidarity variables suggests an answer. One component of these variables deals with the extent of interpersonal conflicts and friction which respondents perceive in the hotel. The refusal to adhere to moral norms, to abide by the "rules of the game," in dealing with others can plausibly be regarded as a source of friction in interpersonal relations. If so, it is understandable that the members of organizations with a high level of Machiavellianism perceive friction and conflict among employees.

Furthermore, the whole flavor of the Mach scale connotes the egoistic pursuit of one's own ambitions and goals. We do not think of the Machiavellian as a person who has much capacity to devote himself to collective goals. Hence we would not expect to find loyalty to the organization a conspicuous feature of any organization whose members are predominantly Machiavellian. Since perceptions of the loyalty of employees constitute one component of the solidarity variables, it makes sense that the Machiavellian level of a hotel correlates negatively with these variables. Also, if most members of an organization are Machiavellian and are therefore relatively inclined to egoistic behavior, employees will understandably not perceive a climate of good will. The Mach index, then, is such that the average index score of employees in a hotel should affect the solidarity of the work milieu and employees' perceptions of that solidarity.

These interpretations, however, leave one feature of the data unexplained.

Table 6.1 indicates that, even when they are in a hotel with a low level of Machiavellianism, the Machiavellians are uninclined to have solidary feelings. The high scorers on the Mach index seem unaffected by the organizational climate. This suggests that a person's SF score may reflect not only the environment in which he is situated but certain personal attributes as well. Since this point merits full discussion, we will return to it in chapter 8.

The Machiavellianism of Top Management

If the level of Machiavellianism among the employees in general affects solidarity, we might next inquire if the Mach scores of management also exert an influence. At first thought, one might readily be inclined to argue that they should. Machiavellianism appears, by its nature, to be an instrumental orientation: the Machiavellian is concerned with the most efficient means of achieving his goals, and he is willing to violate conventional moral norms and "use" other people in order to do so. Therefore we might expect a Machiavellian manager to make special efforts to foster a solidary atmosphere among employees on the theory that such an atmosphere would be conducive to a profitable operation of the hotel. If employees work harmoniously with each other and are loyal to their employer, there ought to be greater efficiency and better service to guests.

To test these notions, we have devised a measure of the Machiavellianism of the top management in each hotel. This measure is simply the mean of the Mach scores of the two leading executives in each hotel. If a hotel has no executive under the general manager who shares in over-all responsibility for managing the organization, then the Machiavellianism of top management is equal to the Mach score of the general manager.

A cross-tabulation of SF scores of the rank and file[4] with the Machiavellianism of the top management indicates that the relationship between the two variables is, at best, a weak one. In a three-by-three table, the

4. In running variables pertaining to management against the SF index, we are interested in ascertaining to what extent the characteristics of management affect the attitudes of other respondents. Consequently, the base in such cross-tabulations includes only rank-and-file respondents (i.e., excludes general managers and assistant managers). This practice has been followed throughout the chapter. In cross-tabulations in which none of the variables refer to management characteristics, however, there is no reason to exclude these two executives from the base, and therefore we have not done so. This distinction between cross-tabulations based only on rank-and-file respondents and cross-tabulations based on all respondents does not apply to the Spearman correlation analysis of organizational variables: the organizational solidarity variable always includes the scores of the general manager and the assistant manager. The rationale for this procedure is that the organizational solidarity variable is intended to characterize each hotel as a whole and therefore should be based on the perceptions of all respondents in the hotel.

percentage difference is only eight points for the first row and three points for the third. The results are similar when we examine the correlation on the organizational level. The Spearman rank-correlation between top management's Mach and organizational solidarity is only .06.

The findings permit two possible interpretations. One is that the Machiavellian is not as adept at managing human relationships as his manipulative ideas might lead us to expect. The other is that Machiavellian managers do not regard high morale and harmonious, cooperative work relations as important—or at least, as of primary importance—in operating a hotel profitably. The second interpretation receives some support from empirical research. One conclusion to be drawn from investigations of group productivity, A. Paul Hare points out, is that "whatever the criteria, productivity in the task area is often achieved only at the expense of member satisfaction in the social-emotional area."[5] If so, solidary relations in a work milieu may not necessarily be a prerequisite for the efficient running of a hotel. In any event, the data at hand do not enable us to test which interpretation is the better of the two.

This should not discourage us, however. The above findings indicate only one thing: that the Machiavellianism of the top management is not *in itself* sufficient to account for variations in SF or in organizational solidarity. This does not mean that management's Machiavellianism is without influence on the latter variables. But to demonstrate this influence, it is necessary to take account of other elements in the work environment. The manner in which the management of an organization affects its subordinates depends not only on the characteristics of management but on the characteristics of the rank and file as well.

The Part Played by Role Expectations

Before we can understand this interplay between the characteristics of the two strata, it is necessary to discuss the link between solidarity and the fulfilment of role expections in an organization.

The term *role expections* commonly refers to the attitudes of actors toward the rights and obligations of each other in a social system.[6] An employer, for

5. See A. P. Hare, *Handbook of Small Group Research* (New York: Free Press, 1962), pp. 374 and 377–78.

6. Surveys of the terminology in this area can be found in the following sources: L. J. Neiman and J. W. Hughes, "The Problem of the Concept of Role: A Resurvey of the Literature," *Social Forces*, 30 (1951):141–49; N. Gross, W. S. Mason, and A. W. McEachern, *Explorations in Role Analysis* (New York: John Wiley and Sons, 1958), chap. 2; and W. J. Goode, "Norm Commitment and Conformity to Role-Status Obligations," *American Journal of Sociology*, 66 (1960):246–58.

example, may expect his employees to produce a certain amount in an hour, to maintain certain minimum standards of quality in output, to avoid excessive absenteeism, and so forth. Not all expectations are based on codified rules or are highly institutionalized. Expectations that reflect self-defined interests, that are based on attitudes acquired during socialization, or that reflect personality characteristics are an important element in any situation. A. W. Gouldner makes this point when he writes:

> The role players in modern organizations must, in some measure, derive their mutual expectations from sources other than codified rules. Consequently, the stability of their relationship is always to some extent contingent upon the extent to which they conform with one another's informal, traditional, and implicit expectations.[7]

Many of the interpretations that follow are based on the assumption that the extent to which the role expectations of a set of individuals are fulfilled has important consequences for the satisfaction that these individuals derive from a given social relationship and for the solidarity of social relations in any organization. This assumption is certainly not tautological. Yet it seems to be taken for granted by social scientists, for we know of no attempt to test it empirically. Perhaps it is too much of a truism to merit such a test. If most employees in an organization expect the manager to be cordial and friendly toward them, yet he is persistently standoffish and dour, no one will be surprised if they become dissatisfied with him and disaffected with the organization.

Demoralization and dissatisfaction with the social relationship are, to be sure, not the only reactions possible in the above situation. The persons involved could change their role expectations. The employees might become accustomed to their boss's ill temper and aloofness and no longer "take it personally." But such changes in expectations are difficult to make and are especially unlikely where the expectations are deeply rooted in the personality. An ambitious woman is not likely to change her values so radically that she becomes contented with a husband whom she views as spineless and unaggressive.

Another procedure people employ for avoiding such frustrating situations is to keep away from others who they know will not, for one reason or another, live up to their expectations. But such selection processes do not, and cannot, always function effectively: the actors in a situation may be initially unaware of the inability of others to gratify their expectations or, once they

7. A. W. Gouldner, "Organizational Analysis," in R. K. Merton et al., eds., *Sociology Today: Problems and Prospects* (New York: Basic Books, 1959), p. 418.

become aware, circumstances may prohibit them from leaving the situation. A person may find his employer inconsiderate, browbeating, deceitful; but he is the main breadwinner in his family and other employment is hard to come by or, being a fainthearted, diffident sort of person, he is apprehensive about looking for another job.

If, then, role expectations in a group or organization are persistently violated and the individuals involved do not change their expectations or do not leave the situation, these individuals will presumably react by becoming estranged from their role relationships and the group will become disaffected. This line of reasoning suggests that if we can identify those structural conditions that affect the extent to which expectations are frustrated or met, we will have a clue to the factors accounting for variations in solidary feelings and in organizational solidarity. One such condition is the degree of consensus about expectations in the organization.

Until recently social scientists usually assumed that role expectations command wide agreement among the members of an organization. Thus N. Gross and his associates remark that

> . . . the postulate of consensus is still enmeshed in the analyses of many students of social behavior. Since their analyses assume consensus on role definitions among members of a group or "society," they have ignored its possible significance as a variable for social science inquiry.[8]

As we shall see later on, the extent of agreement concerning role expectations is indeed of critical importance in interpreting some of the statistical relationships we have found.

Where there is little consensus, we shall speak of role conflict.[9] If A believes that B should act in one way but B believes that he should act in another, B may act in accordance with his own wishes—in which case A's expectations will, by definition, have been frustrated. Or B may, because of A's superior power or for some other reason, conform to A's expectations,

8. Gross, Mason, and McEachern, *Explorations in Role Analysis*, p. 42.

9. The phrase *role conflict* is used here in a somewhat different sense than it is normally used in the literature. Most writers employ it as a general label for a variety of conditions. Thus it may include the conflict a person finds himself in by virtue of holding several positions, the expectations of one position requiring him to do something which is inconsistent with the expectations of another. It usually also includes situations in which occupants of different positions hold incompatible expectations toward an actor. There is no need for us to list all the meanings that have been subsumed under the term. It will suffice to say that, for our purposes, role conflict refers to any situation in which there is disagreement among the participants about the expectations that should apply to one or more actors in the situation. In using the term in this way, we are deliberately ignoring distinctions which other writers have found useful but which are not relevant here.

thus acting contrary to his own wishes. In this case, it is B's expectations that will have been violated. So when members of an organization disagree about values and expectations, the expectations of some of the members are likely to be frustrated, the result being interpersonal friction and demoralization.[10]

Is it possible to specify any conditions that favor such cleavages in values and expectations? We will argue that one cause of role conflict is differences in personality characteristics. This contention, however, rests on the assumption that personality characteristics are a determinant of the expectations that a person has in any situation. We must therefore address ourselves to this point first.

An individual's personality may affect the expectations he exhibits in a role relationship in two respects. In the first place, personality variables may be social in the sense of referring primarily to the way a person acts in his relations with other people. When we say that a person is dominant, for example, we mean that he exhibits the qualities of ascendance and forcefulness in interpersonal situations. Such a person expects other people to let him take the lead and to follow him. This is also true of a personality characteristic such as the need for affiliation. A person who has a strong need for affiliation will naturally expect others to be cordial and friendly.

Personality characteristics are also linked to role expectations in a second way (which perhaps overlaps with the first), for they may entail commitment to certain values. The person low on the F scale, for instance, places a positive value on ethnic tolerance. This value will come into play in situations involving members of minority groups. Thus such a person will expect his friends to avoid derogatory remarks about Negroes and will expect his neighbors not to discriminate against Jewish families when selling their homes.

These remarks are admittedly more a catalogue of examples than a systematic exposition of how personality characteristics are linked to role expectations. Nevertheless, they do serve to suggest that such a link exists. And if so, it is reasonable to conjecture that sharp personality differences among members of an organization may be manifested in conflicts about role expectations.[11]

10. For a small group study lending support to this argument, see D. Marquis et al., "A Social Psychological Study of the Decision-Making Conference," in H. Guetzkow, ed., *Groups, Leadership, and Men* (Pittsburgh: Carnegie Press, 1951), pp. 55–67.

11. Evidence for this conjecture is to be found in several studies. See, for example, R. B. Cattell et al., "The Dimensions of Syntality"; and W. C. Schutz, "What Makes Groups Productive?" *Human Relations*, 8 (1955):429–65. Obviously not all personality differences entail role conflict. Indeed, some differences involve complementary characteristics and are therefore functional for the activities of a group. Winch's theory of

The argument can be summed up in the following propositions. (1) Personality characteristics comprise one determinant of role expectations. (2) Therefore, marked differences in certain personality characteristics among members of an organization may give rise to conflicts in role expectations. (3) As a result of role conflict in the day-to-day activities of members, the role expectations of many members may be frustrated. (4) A likely reaction to this frustration is interpersonal friction and demoralization. A corollary of these four points is: Organizations whose members show marked differences in certain personality characteristics will exhibit unsolidary social relations and low morale.

A few small group studies that we have seen corroborate the last proposition. In one of them, E. F. Gross obtained measurements on nine groups set up for experimental purposes, each consisting of five Harvard freshmen.[12] The groups were scored on "compatibility" with respect to certain personality variables, one of which was "affection." Groups highly compatible on this variable consisted of members who showed similarities in the degree of intimacy that they preferred in their relations with other people. Group compatibility was, in turn, viewed in relation to each group's score on "cohesiveness," which was obtained by summing the scores of group members on a Guttman-type scale. The items in this scale, for the most part, measured the member's satisfaction with the group, with its activities, and with the other members of the group. There was a rank-order correlation of .40 between group scores on compatibility on the affection variable and group scores on cohesiveness.

W. C. Schutz's interpretation of this type of compatibility is based on what we have called role expectations. Compatibility, he writes, means that "people must *agree* on the same degree of closeness of personal feelings, of expression of confidences, and so forth. . . ." Incompatibility occurs "when one person *likes* to be personal, intimate, and confiding, while the other does not *want* to discuss personal matters."[13] Thus, role conflict

---

mate selection in marriage is based on the notion that individuals with complementary qualities or "needs" actually seek out each other as prospective mates. The theory follows from the assumption that complementariness in psychic qualities, which may include differences on the same personality dimensions, contributes to the psychological gratification of each of the spouses in a marriage. See R. F. Winch et al., "The Theory of Complementary Needs in Mate Selection: An Analytic and Descriptive Study," *American Sociological Review*, 19 (1954): 241–49.

12. E. F. Gross, "An Empirical Study of the Concepts of Cohesiveness and Compatibility" (Honors Thesis, Harvard University, 1952), described in W. C. Schutz, *FIRO: A Three-Dimensional Theory of Interpersonal Behavior* (New York: Rinehart, 1958), pp. 137–39.

13. Ibid., p. 111. Italics added.

appears to have mediated the effects of incompatibility on "cohesiveness" in the above experiment.[14]

The Incongruity Variables

HIERARCHICAL INCONGRUITY

Through an extended digression, we have arrived at the proposition that incongruence in certain personality characteristics renders the members of an organization prone to role conflict and thereby to unsolidary social relations and low morale. This proposition suggests that, if the Machiavellianism score of top management alone does not affect SF and organizational solidarity, perhaps this variable should be taken in conjunction with the Mach scores of the rank and file. In order to do this, we have devised a measure which we call "hierarchical incongruity." This variable is simply the arithmetic difference between the mean Mach of the top management and the mean Mach of all other respondents in a hotel. The version of this measure that is employed here has three categories: (a) large difference, with top management higher than all other respondents in a hotel; (b) small difference; and (c) large difference, with rank and file higher than top management.

When we cross-tabulate hierarchical incongruity with SF, the results are striking (table 6.2). The table reveals a definite relationship: respondents from hotels with low incongruity are much higher on SF than respondents from hotels with high incongruity. Moreover, the two high incongruity categories differ from each other in respect to the proportion high on SF by only three percentage points. Whether the top management or the rank and file is higher on the Mach scale appears to make little difference: respondents will be equally low on solidary feelings regardless of the type of incongruity.

Computing a Spearman correlation would not be appropriate for the hierarchical incongruity variable since its measurement is on a nominal scale, not on an ordinal scale. Consequently, we have cast the organizational data into a two-by-two table with low versus high organizational solidarity as one variable and the two high incongruity categories versus the small difference category as the other. When the Fisher Exact Probability Test is calculated on the frequencies in this table, the probability that the two

14. A second study intimating a relationship between opposing personality characteristics and group demoralization is W. Haythorn et al., "The Effects of Varying Combinations of Authoritarian and Equalitarian Groups and Followers," *Journal of Abnormal and Social Psychology*, 53 (1956):210–19.

TABLE 6.2
SF SCORES OF RANK-AND-FILE RESPONDENTS BY HIERARCHICAL INCONGRUITY

SF Scores of Rank and File	*Hierarchical Incongruity*		
	Management Higher	*Small Difference*	*Rank and File Higher*
Low	32%	17%	34%
Medium	38	22	39
High	30	61	27
	100	100	100
	(53)	(36)	(77)

$\chi^2 = 13.275$; df = 4; $.025 > p > .01$.

variables are statistically independent of each other is .05 or less.[15] Thus the relationship between hierarchical incongruity and solidarity shows up on the organizational as well as on the contextual level.

We have demonstrated that a disparity between the Machiavellianism of the top management and that of rank-and-file respondents in a hotel is associated with low scores on the SF index. The intervening process, according to our interpretation, is a lack of consensus with respect to role expectations with the consequent frustration of expectations for many members of the organization. Unfortunately we have no direct measures of role conflict or of the frustration of expectations and therefore cannot test this interpretation with the data at hand.

The absence of direct measures of role expectations also means that we are unable to specify in detail the character of the role conflict associated with high incongruity. Some of our earlier remarks, however, suggest that the issues around which there is cleavage between the Machiavellians and the non-Machiavellians probably have little to do with formal, codified rules. It is not likely that the antagonists differ on such things as the need to be at work on time or the necessity for neatness in dress. The conflicting expectations probably refer to the more informal, less tangible aspects of the work milieu, to behaviors that cannot be defined in a clear-cut fashion.

Role conflict may take such forms as the following. Rank-and-file employees who are non-Machiavellian may feel that Machiavellian managers are "inconsiderate," that they try to exploit them by squeezing every ounce of work from them, that they are "untrustworthy" in that they do not keep their word. Machiavellian managers, on the other hand, may find that non-Machiavellian employees fail to take advantage of every opportunity to encourage guests to spend money; that they are not "aggressive" and

15. See S. Siegal, *Non-Parametric Statistics for the Behavioral Sciences* (New York: McGraw-Hill Book Company, 1956), pp. 96–104, for a description of the Fisher Exact Probability Test.

"shrewd" enough in dealing with guests. Or take the situation of a non-Machiavellian manager who has to deal with Machiavellian employees. He may feel that they are not really interested in their work, being in the hotel only to earn a dollar, and that they take every opportunity they can to shirk their responsibilities. Machiavellian employees may view a low Mach manager as a "sucker" to be taken advantage of or they may feel that he is naïve to expect them to be loyal to their employer when the latter pays them "peanuts."

These examples are, of course, all hypothetical. We do not know precisely what forms the conflict in values and expectations takes. Indeed, the actors themselves would perhaps be unaware of the exact nature of the conflict. If we questioned them, they might be conscious that there is interpersonal friction in the work milieu, but only with great difficulty and after considerable probing, if even then, could they articulate the basis of it. Or they might voice a few vague complaints without realizing that basic value differences lay at the root of the problem.

MACHIAVELLIAN HETEROGENEITY

If incongruity between top management and the rank and file on the Mach variable is conducive to role conflict, what about incongruence among employees in general? Conflicting expectations need not be a matter of top management versus all others. The split may take a different form, one in which opposing orientations each draw adherents from rank-and-file personnel. We can conceive of two types of hotels—one where the personnel are fairly homogeneous with respect to Machiavellianism, the other where great variability exists in Mach scores among the employees. This second incongruity variable, which we shall call Machiavellian heterogeneity, can be operationally defined as the standard deviation in Mach scores among the rank-and-file employees of a hotel.

TABLE 6.3
SF SCORES OF RANK-AND-FILE RESPONDENTS BY MACHIAVELLIAN HETEROGENEITY

SF Scores of Rank and File	*Machiavellian Heterogeneity*	
	Low	*High*
Low	27%	31%
Medium	28	39
High	45	31
	100	100
	(67)	(99)

$\chi^2 = 3.407$; df = 2; $.25 > p > .10$.

This variable relates to SF roughly as we would expect from the previous discussion: respondents in the more heterogeneous hotels are relatively low on SF. The correlation, however, is not large (table 6.3). The results are no more striking on the organizational level; the Spearman rank-correlation between Machiavellian heterogeneity and organization solidarity is only −.16. Although the statistical relationships are modest, they are nevertheless in the predicted direction.

When we run both incongruity variables simultaneously against the SF index, we find that the previous data understate the influence of Machiavellian heterogeneity. As table 6.4 indicates, the latter variable manifests its full effect only in hotels with low hierarchical incongruity. Where, on the other hand, hierarchical incongruity is high, the heterogeneity variable has little effect; indeed, the correlation is reversed, heterogeneous hotels having a slightly higher proportion with solidary feelings than homogeneous hotels.

TABLE 6.4
PERCENTAGE OF RANK-AND-FILE RESPONDENTS SCORING HIGH ON SF BY HIERARCHICAL INCONGRUITY AND BY MACHIAVELLIAN HETEROGENEITY

Machiavellian Heterogeneity	*Hierarchical Incongruity*	
	Low	*High*
Low	59% (39)	24% (41)
High	25% (28)	33% (58)

A vs. B: $\chi^2 = 8.80$; df = 1; $p < .005$. C vs. D: $\chi^2 = .29$; df = 1; $.75 > p > .50$. A vs. C: $\chi^2 = 6.38$; df = 1; $.025 > p > .01$. B vs. D: $\chi^2 = .97$; df = 1; $.50 > p > .25$.

Table 6.4 also reveals that hierarchical incongruity influences solidary feelings only under certain circumstances. If the heterogeneity variable is high, incongruity makes little difference; the correlation, in fact, is somewhat positive. It is only when hotels are homogeneous that incongruity operates as expected.

One last point should be made. If a hotel is already incongruous in one respect, its becoming incongruous in a second respect will not depress the solidary feelings of the rank and file any further. Respondents in hotels with both kinds of incongruity are not, by and large, any lower on the SF index than respondents in hotels with only one kind of incongruity. It follows that a high level of solidary feelings exists only if a hotel is low on both incongruity variables.

In conclusion, the findings on the two incongruity variables—hierarchical incongruity and Machiavellian heterogeneity—are consistent with the argument that personality differences in a work group can give rise to role conflict which, in turn, leads to the frustration of role expectations and thereby disrupts the solidarity of the group. But incongruity is not the only condition that conduces to the frustration of role expectations. Some other conditions will be dealt with in the next chapter.

CHAPTER 7

The Personality Characteristics of Management

WE PREVIOUSLY inquired how the Machiavellianism of management impinges on solidarity in the work milieu. Since our study also includes other personality variables, it may be worthwhile to explore whether management's standing on these affects solidarity.[1]

The Dominance of Top Management

One such variable consists of items taken from the Dominance scale of the Edwards Personal Preference Schedule. A person who scores high on this set of items likes "to supervise and to direct the actions of other people," to "be one of the leaders in the organizations and groups to which I belong," and to "make the decisions about what we are going to do." Judging by the face content, this variable measures the propensity of a person to be ascendant and to assume control of matters in his relations with others—in short, to be "boss." To derive the dominance score of top management, we have calculated the mean of the dominance scores for the general manager and the number two executive.

When we cross-tabulate management dominance with SF, a correlation does show up (table 7.1). The figures reveal an inverse relationship in which the higher top management is on dominance, the lower its employees tend to be on the SF index. The correlation, though, is only a moderate one. The modest strength of the correlation is confirmed on the organizational level, where the Spearman correlation between management dominance and work solidarity is .28.

1. There are two excellent sources that review studies dealing with the effects of the characteristics of leadership or supervisory personnel upon group functioning. In the field of organizational research, see P. M. Blau and W. R. Scott, *Formal Organizations: A Comparative Approach* (San Francisco: Chandler Publishing Co., 1962), pp. 145–48. For small group studies, see A. P. Hare, *Handbook of Small Group Research* (New York: Free Press, 1962), pp. 310–36. A classic small group experiment in this area is R. White and R. Lippitt, "Leader Behavior and Member Reaction in Three 'Social Climates,'" in D. Cartwright and A. Zander, eds., *Group Dynamics: Research and Theory*, 2d ed. (Evanston, Ill.: Row, Peterson and Company, 1960), pp. 527–53.

TABLE 7.1
SF SCORES OF RANK-AND-FILE RESPONDENTS BY MANAGEMENT DOMINANCE

SF Scores of Rank and File	*Management Dominance*		
	Low	*Medium*	*High*
Low	18%	33%	36%
Medium	41	31	36
High	41	36	27
	100	100	100
	(49)	(84)	(33)

$\chi^2 = 4.908$; df = 4; $.50 > p > .25$.

How are we to interpret these correlations? We could argue as follows: People who score high on dominance like to exert influence and exercise leadership. But liking to do these things is not the same as being effective in doing them. Indeed, a person who agrees with most of the dominance items is probably one whom others regard as "bossy." He is not simply dominant; he is domineering. If so, the inverse correlations noted above could be explained by the adverse effects which dominance has on rank-and-file employees. The latter react to the domineering, "bossy" behavior of the managers by increased interpersonal friction, diminished loyalty to the hotel, and reduced morale.

The above interpretation has a certain plausibility. Nevertheless, when we introduce an additional variable into the analysis, this interpretation proves to be oversimplified and inadequate. Table 7.2 reveals a marked

TABLE 7.2
PERCENTAGE OF RANK-AND-FILE RESPONDENTS HIGH ON SF BY HIERARCHICAL INCONGRUITY AND BY MANAGEMENT DOMINANCE

Management Dominance	*Hierarchical Incongruity*		
	Management Higher	*Small Difference*	*Rank and File Higher*
Low	42% (24)	43% (14)	36% (25)
High	21% (29)	73% (22)	23% (52)

A vs. B vs. C: $\chi^2 = .17$; df = 2; $.95 > p > .90$. D vs. E vs. F: $\chi^2 = 21.59$; df = 2; $p < .005$. A vs. D: $\chi^2 = 2.18$; df = 1; $.25 > p > .10$. B vs. E: $\chi^2 = 3.$; df = 1; $.10 > p > .05$. C vs. F: $\chi^2 = .59$; df = 1; $.90 > p > .75$.

interaction effect. Our first table was partially correct: high dominance on the part of management does result in lowered SF scores. But this is true only where there is hierarchical incongruity. Where there is little or no incongruity, management dominance has the opposite effect; it raises the proportion scoring high on SF. Moreover, introducing hierarchical incongruity as a variable yields correlations that are higher than the original correlation between management dominance and perceived solidarity.

What do these findings signify? Dominance refers to the inclination to take the lead. In the context of conflicting values and conflicting role expectations between top management and rank and file, dominance only aggravates the conflict; it means that management actively seeks to impose its values and its expectations even though these may run counter to the values and expectations of the rank and file. In the context of low incongruity, on the other hand, dominance has a different significance. Where the rank and file do not view management as having alien values and expectations, management's exercise of authority does not require that their values and role expectations be violated. Indeed, management's forceful exercise of authority is probably accepted as a natural thing. It accords with the definitions of employer-employee relations prevailing in our society, and where this exercise is not threatening to employees, they will regard it as natural.

Also noteworthy in table 7.2 is what happens to the incongruity variable when the dominance of management is controlled for. If management consists of personality types that are low on dominance, hierarchical incongruity has practically no effect on the solidary feelings of the rank and file. If management is not inclined to force its values and expectations on the rank and file, the existence of role conflict does not lower solidary feelings. The influence of the incongruity variable is felt only in hotels in which the management is high on dominance. Evidently the existence of disparate values and expectations between the leadership and the rank and file does not produce unsolidary feelings unless the leadership has a propensity for imposing its expectations on the rest of the members.

The preceding two tables are instructive in that they underline a point we made earlier: viewing a psychological characteristic of one segment of an organization in isolation from the social context can be misleading. We saw that this was the case with the Machiavellianism of management since this characteristic could not be properly analyzed apart from the Machiavellian level prevailing among the personnel of a hotel. Now we have seen that the same point applies to another management characteristic. The effects of the level of dominance of top management are not the same in all organizational contexts. Where there is an incompatibility of personalities and conflicting expectations, management dominance has one effect. Where personality tendencies and role expectations are in harmony, the effect is entirely different. In this instance, organizational functioning does not depend solely on a psychological characteristic of management—but on this characteristic taken in conjunction with a social factor. Viewing either the psychological characteristic or the social factor alone distorts our understanding. They must be viewed conjointly, for they operate conjointly.

Sympathy and the Need for Social Approval Among Managers

For a further illustration of this point, let us consider management's position on the measures of the looking-glass process included in the present study. As the reader will recall, we have two indices relevant to this process. One of these, the index of sympathy, presumably taps an individual's propensity for "feeling with others," for imagining the reactions and attitudes of other people toward different situations. The second index, that of the need for social approval, seems to gauge a person's sensitivity to the approval and disapproval of other people. Although both of these indices are psychological in the sense that they measure personality tendencies of individuals, they nonetheless have relevance to concerns that are customarily considered sociological. From a sociological perspective, the looking-glass process deals with a person's orientation toward role expectations. Sympathy, it can be argued, measures the varying propensities for affectively experiencing the expectations of others; and the need for social approval refers to how sensitive a person is to role expectations, how psychologically uncomfortable he is likely to feel if he violates these expectations.

Thus conceived, the looking-glass process can be related to the arguments we presented earlier concerning the part role expectations play in solidary social relations and morale. For, if our interpretation of the looking-glass process is correct, that process would exert a strong influence on the ability of management to meet the role expectations of the rank and file. Management that possesses a high degree of sympathy supposedly has a greater emotional appreciation of what these expectations are, and such appreciation would seem to be an important element in the ability to meet expectations. Likewise, management that is high on the need for social approval is more likely, because of its greater sensitivity to the disapproval of other individuals, to conform to these expectations.

In order to test this line of reasoning, we have calculated the mean score of top management on these two variables. The correlations of management's position on them with solidarity seems to bear out our arguments. Table 7.3 tells us about the relation of management's score on the need for social approval to SF. Respondents from hotels in which the management has a great need for social approval are comparatively likely to be high on SF.

The correlation is fairly strong. The statistical association at the organizational level, however, is not quite as strong as we might expect from the contextual findings since the Spearman rank-correlation between management's need for social approval and organizational solidarity is .21.

TABLE 7.3
SF SCORES OF RANK-AND-FILE RESPONDENTS BY THE NEED FOR SOCIAL APPROVAL OF TOP MANAGEMENT

SF Scores of Rank and File	*Management's Need for Social Approval*		
	Low	*Medium*	*High*
Low	34%	34%	17%
Medium	39	34	29
High	27	32	55
	100	100	100
	(74)	(50)	(42)

$\chi^2 = 10.081$; df = 4; $.05 > p > .025$.

The findings involving the sympathy of management are even more striking than those for the need for social approval. Table 7.4 indicates that the more sympathetic top management is, the higher the SF scores of the other personnel tend to be. The results are equally impressive for the organizational correlations. The Spearman coefficient for the relationship of the sympathy of management to organizational solidarity is .46.

TABLE 7.4
SF SCORES OF RANK-AND-FILE RESPONDENTS BY THE SYMPATHY OF TOP MANAGEMENT

SF Scores of Rank and File	*Management's Sympathy*		
	Low	*Medium*	*High*
Low	36%	36%	14%
Medium	40	35	30
High	24	29	56
	100	100	100
	(50)	(66)	(50)

$\chi^2 = 15.163$; df = 4; $p < .005$.

Given these results, we might be content to accept a formula such as the following: The looking-glass process fosters an ability on the part of management to meet the role expectations of employees and, for this reason, is conducive to solidarity in the work environment. Such an interpretation says, in effect, that this process operates in the same way regardless of the organizational context. Our previous experience, however, has taught us to be wary of any such notion.

When dealing with the looking-glass process, moreover, we have even more reason to be cautious. Reviewing a number of studies on the relation of accurate social perception to individual and group effectiveness, I. D. Steiner points out that the findings are mixed.[2] Some investigations show perceptual accuracy to be functional, but there are others which fail to show this. From these mixed findings he conjectures that the effects of accuracy are contingent on social conditions.

At least one empirical study bears out this general view. S. Stryker investigated role-taking ability in relation to social adjustment between different generations in a family unit.[3] The sample consisted of forty-six family units, each of which comprised a young married couple and the parents of one of the spouses. Role-taking ability was measured by the extent of agreement between A's predictions about B's responses to a scale on traditionalism in family matters, and B's actual responses to the scale. The independent variable was the role-taking ability of the two older members of each family unit (the parental generation); the dependent variable was their "adjustment" to the young couple.[4]

Contrary to his initial predictions, Stryker found that parents who were accurate in role-taking had made a poorer adjustment than parents who were relatively unskilled at it. In order to account for this, he introduced the concept of "vulnerability"—a concept which, though not explicitly defined, apparently referred to any condition that would aggravate the adjustment of the parents to the young couple in each family unit. The study included three separate measures of this concept: (1) the extent of agreement on a traditionalism scale between each person and each member of the other generation in the family unit, (2) the degree of parental dependence on the members of the younger generation, and (3) the score of each of the parents on the traditionalism scale. Family units with low agreement, high dependence, or high traditionalism were assumed to be highly vulnerable.

Stryker's principal finding was that among family units that exhibited high vulnerability, parents who were poor in role-taking ability showed better adjustment than those who were proficient at it. Among family units with

2. See I. D. Steiner, "Interpersonal Behavior as Influenced by Accuracy of Social Perception," in E. P. Hollander and R. G. Hunt, eds., *Current Perspectives in Social Psychology*, 2d ed. (New York: Oxford University Press, 1967), pp. 266–71.

3. See S. Stryker, "Role-Taking Accuracy and Adjustment," in M. B. Sussman, ed., *Sourcebook in Marriage and the Family*, 2d ed. (Boston: Houghton Mifflin, 1963), pp. 385–93.

4. The author unfortunately specified neither what he meant by "adjustment" nor the content of the items used to measure it.

low vulnerability, on the other hand, the relationship tended in the other direction: the mean adjustment scores were higher for accurate role-takers than for inaccurate role-takers, although the difference attained statistical significance only in the case of nontraditional parents.

In a previous chapter, we argued that accuracy of person perception must be distinguished from sympathy since the latter is only one of many factors possibly entering into person perception. Nonetheless, the results of this study are suggestive. For they raise the possibility that the effects of the looking-glass process may depend on certain characteristics of the social relationship; more specifically, that where conditions favor strain among the members of a group, the process may not lessen the strain and may even intensify it.

Thus both our experience in analyzing other management characteristics and substantive considerations make it advisable to ascertain if sympathy and the need for social approval on the part of the management correlate with the solidary feelings of the rank and file in the same way regardless of the social context. Our previous analysis indicated three environmental conditions that affect solidarity—the Machiavellian level, the heterogeneity of Machiavellianism, and hierarchical incongruity. We have held each of these constant while running the two management variables against the SF index. Of the six cross-tabulations that result from this procedure, only one, table 7.5, is presented here.

TABLE 7.5
PERCENTAGE OF RANK-AND-FILE RESPONDENTS HIGH ON THE SF INDEX BY MANAGEMENT'S NEED FOR SOCIAL APPROVAL AND BY HIERARCHICAL INCONGRUITY

Hierarchical Incongruity	*Management's Need for Social Approval*	
	Low	*High*
Low	9% (11)	46% (69)
High	29% (66)	35% (20)

A vs. B: $\chi^2 = 5.09$; df = 1; .025 > p > .01. C vs. D: $\chi^2 = .01$; df = 1; .95 > p > .90. A vs. C: $\chi^2 = 13.72$; df = 1; p < .005. B vs. D: $\chi^2 = .52$; df = 1; .50 > p > .25.

When we control for each of the organizational variables affecting solidary feelings, we find that in general the effect of management's position on the looking-glass process depends on the organizational context. Where the environment fosters unsolidary feelings on the part of the rank and file, high scores on sympathy and on the need for social approval tend to show little effect or their effect is to lower SF scores. On the other hand, high scores are functional for solidary feelings where the organizational context is already favorable to the development of such feelings. (This pattern clearly holds in five of the tables and exists in the sixth as well, though it is not as marked here.)

The most plausible interpretation of these findings, it seems to us, is that emotional appreciation of the expectations of others and sensitivity to these expectations do not in themselves signify that role expectations will be fulfilled with high frequency. If, for example, there is a cleavage between the moral orientation of management and that of the rank and file, as presumably exists when there is a large amount of hierarchical incongruity, a high level of sympathy on the part of management will mean that the latter has greater affective awareness of this cleavage. But such awareness does not foster a greater inclination to meet expectations, since these are based on values at variance with one's own.

Similarly one can argue that managers who are sensitive to approval are likely to become emotionally disconcerted in the face of expectations that are contrary to their own values. The effect of their sensitivity is not to promote greater conformity to the opposing role expectations but to create an inner uneasiness and possibly to strengthen the resolve to resist values they find odious. It appears that only where the role expectations of the other actors in a situation are based on values that are consistent with one's own moral orientation that the looking-glass process will conduce to the fulfilling of these expectations. This interpretation applies to the hierarchical incongruity variable. Other interpretations, similar in some respects to this one, could be made for the other environmental factors that condition the effects of management's need for social approval and management's sympathy.

A NOTE ON THE VALIDITY OF THE INDICES OF THE LOOKING-GLASS PROCESS

The items comprising the indices of the looking-glass process originally come from personality scales intended to measure other variables. The items referring to the need for social approval are from the Lykken Anxiety Scale. Those for the index of sympathy are drawn from the need Intraception scale of the Edwards Personal Preference Schedule. In both cases the main evidence for the validity of the items is their face content.

In addition, Lykken's findings on sociopaths are consistent with our conceptualization of the Lykken items employed in the index of the need for social approval.[5] One of the defining characteristics of sociopathy is the

5. See D. T. Lykken, "A Study of Anxiety in the Sociopathic Personality," in T. R. Sarbin, ed., *Studies in Behavior Pathology* (New York: Holt, Rinehart, and Winston, 1961), pp. 149–54.

failure of conscience to operate in an individual. Following Cooley, we have argued that one factor in this failure is a person's inability to react with shame to the disapproval that other people have of his behavior. If our interpretation of the Lykken items is correct and they do, in fact, measure this inability to react with shame, we would naturally expect the sociopaths to score comparatively low on the Lykken scale. Lykken's investigation bears out this expectation. His data, however, do not unambiguously confirm our conceptualization since they are also consistent with Lykken's own contention that anxiety is the variable measured by his scale.

The data concerning the looking-glass process as it operates on the management level constitute further evidence for the validity of our indices. One species of validity is construct validity.[6] Once we have developed an index, we may expect to find certain correlations between it and other variables on the basis of our conceptualization of it or on the basis of a body of theory. If we do, in fact, find these correlations, such findings constitute an indirect sort of validating evidence.

Our original intention in developing the indices gauging sympathy and the need for social approval was to test hypotheses about their relationship to Machiavellianism. We have, in addition, found that they relate to other variables (SF and organizational solidarity) in a way that "makes sense" theoretically and conceptually. According to our interpretation of the indices of the looking-glass process, the leadership of an organization that is high on these indices should have a greater sensitivity, and conform more often, to the role expectations of the rank and file than leadership that is low on these indices. The rank and file in organizations with such leadership should therefore have greater solidary feelings, and such organizations should score higher on organizational solidarity. And this is precisely what we find. Furthermore, a study employing a measure of role-taking intimated that where a role relationship is vulnerable to maladjustment, the looking-glass process may not mitigate the maladjustment and may even aggravate it. The findings here are in accord with this intimation, too.

That our indices relate to other variables in a way that is suggested by our conceptualization of them and by findings from a previous study constitutes an additional bit of evidence for their validity.

The Aggression of Top Management

An important component of our measures of solidarity deals with interpersonal friction and conflict in the hotel. One set of items asks the number

6. See L. J. Cronbach and P. E. Meehl, "Construct Validity in Psychological Tests," *Psychological Bulletin*, 52 (1955):281–302.

of "disputes or quarrels" the respondent has "heard of or personally witnessed" in the three weeks prior to his taking the questionnaire. Another item inquires about "tension and friction among the employees with whom you work" during periods of heavy business. Given this element of friction and conflict in our dependent variables, one would naturally expect that a manager's methods of handling aggression would affect solidarity in the work milieu. A manager who, by temperament, manifests a high level of aggression toward others would be likely, so the argument would run, to become embroiled with other employees.

We have two indices dealing with an individual's mode of handling aggression. One of these, which consists of items from the need Abasement scale of the Edwards Personal Preference Schedule, measures the tendency to direct aggression "inward" in the form of self-blame, guilt, and feelings of depression. The second index comprises items from the need Aggression scale of the EPPS. It taps the propensity to direct hostility "outward": the high scorer reports that, at times, he feels like "telling people off," "getting revenge," "throwing and breaking things," "attacking points of view" contrary to those of the respondent, and so forth. The mean score of the top management in each hotel was calculated for both of these indices. This yielded two measures—the abasement of the top management and the aggression of the top management.

In light of the above discussion, we can predict that there will be a positive correlation between the abasement of top management and the two solidarity variables and that there will be a negative correlation between the aggression of top management and solidarity. The first prediction is confirmed, though the statistical association is only moderate.[7] Respondents in hotels whose management scores high on abasement are somewhat more likely to exhibit solidary feelings than respondents in hotels whose management scores low. A parallel finding emerges on the collective level: the Spearman correlation between the abasement of management and organizational solidarity is .20, a coefficient which is not as high as most of the other Spearman coefficients that we have presented.

When we turn to the aggression of top management we obtain some curious findings. The correlation revealed by table 7.6 is strong—but it is in the opposite direction from that predicted! The solidary feelings of the rank and file vary directly with management's aggression, so that the higher management is on aggression, the higher its employees tend to score on the SF index. The same pattern obtains for the rank correlation of management's aggression with organizational solidarity, the coefficient being .28.

7. The relevant data are not shown in the text.

TABLE 7.6
SF SCORES OF RANK-AND-FILE RESPONDENTS BY THE AGGRESSION OF TOP MANAGEMENT

SF Scores of Rank and File	*Management's Aggression*			
	Low	*Medium-Low*	*Medium-High*	*High*
Low	38%	32%	19%	28%
Medium	46	34	36	26
High	16	34	44	47
	100	100	100	100
	(37)	(50)	(36)	(43)

$\chi^2 = 10.814$; df = 6; $.10 > p > .05$.

These findings are baffling. They present something of a paradox, moreover, since the aggression variable does "work" when it is used to analyze the effects of respondents' own predispositions upon their solidary feelings. But this is getting ahead of our story somewhat. The discussion will return to the aggression variable in Chapter 8, where we will attempt a partial explanation of the data presented here.

Intrarank Conflict and Interrank Conflict

In his discussion of cohesion in organizational settings, Amitai Etzioni makes a distinction between peer cohesion and hierarchical cohesion.[8] The former refers to cohesive bonds among individuals of the same rank in an organization, the latter to cohesive relations among individuals of different rank, such as management personnel and rank-and-file personnel. Although Etzioni's concept of cohesion is somewhat different from the concept of solidarity that we are using, the distinction is nevertheless applicable here. Unfortunately, this distinction was not central in our thinking when we drafted the items for the SF index, so that it cannot be applied to the index as a whole or to most of its components.

There is one component, however, that lends itself readily to this distinction. In asking about disputes and quarrels among employees, we presented three separate items to the respondent, two of which fit in with the distinction. One inquires about disputes and quarrels among nonmanagerial personnel in the three weeks prior to the administration of the questionnaire and is thus a measure of perceived solidarity among personnel of the same rank. Asking for virtually the same information about conflict between man-

8. See A. Etzioni, *A Comparative Study of Complex Organization* (New York: Free Press, 1961), p. 177.

agerial and nonmanagerial employees, the other item refers to perceived solidarity among people of different ranks.

Here we will present the correlations of these two items with three environmental variables. These are variables with which one or both of the items show fairly high correlations. Table 7.7 presents the cross-tabulations

TABLE 7.7
PERCENTAGE OF RANK-AND-FILE RESPONDENTS PERCEIVING NO QUARRELS BY HIERARCHICAL INCONGRUITY

	Hierarchical Incongruity		
Percent of Rank and File Perceiving No Quarrels	*Management Higher*	*Small Difference*	*Rank and File Higher*
Between Management and Nonmanagement	58% (53)	78% (37)	58% (78)
	$\chi^2 = 5.34$; df = 2; $.10 > p > .05$.		
Among Nonmanagerial Personnel	62% (53)	78% (37)	51% (78)
	$\chi^2 = 6.89$; df = 2; $.05 > p > .025$.		

for hierarchical incongruity. Paradoxically, the statistical association is somewhat stronger for quarrels among nonmanagerial personnel than for quarrels between management and nonmanagerial employees. Assuming the correctness of our previous interpretations, this fact suggests that role conflict between management and rank and file has less effect on perceived social relations between these two strata than on perceived relations among members of the lower stratum. Before discussing the implications of this, let us present the data for the other two environmental variables.

Table 7.8 lists the tau-beta coefficients for the cross-tabulations involving the dominance of top management and the sympathy of top management. Again we obtain a paradoxical finding: the dominance of management has greater influence on perceived conflict among rank-and-file employees than on perceived conflict between the two ranks. If "bossiness" on the part of an executive affects his perceived relations with the rank and file, it affects the perceived relations among members of the rank and file even more. A slightly different picture emerges when we examine management's sympathy. This variable shows a marked effect on the amount of perceived conflict, but it correlates with the two quarrel items to about the same extent. That is, a manager's sympathy has approximately the same influence on perceived

TABLE 7.8
TAU-BETA CORRELATION COEFFICIENTS FOR CROSS-TABULATIONS OF NUMBER OF QUARRELS WITH MANAGEMENT CHARACTERISTICS

	Quarrels	
	Between Management and Nonmanagement	*Among Nonmanagement*
Top Management's Dominance	.09	.16
Top Management's Sympathy	−.26	−.25

relations between the two strata as on perceived relations among members of the lower stratum. It thus differs from the other two environmental variables. What is perhaps even more remarkable, however, is that, although perceived quarrels among nonexecutive personnel are not affected to a greater degree than those between the two ranks, they are *no less* affected.

All three of the above variables involve relations between top management and the rank and file. Hierarchical incongruity, according to our interpretation, indirectly reflects the amount of role conflict between the two strata. The degree of dominance exhibited by executives measures how domineering they are in their relations with lower-level personnel. And the sympathy variable, we have argued, refers to the degree to which management is affectively aware of the role expectations of employees. Hence each variable seems to tap some aspect of social relations between the two ranks. Yet their effect is reflected no less in perceived conflict among members of the lower rank than in perceived conflict between the two ranks. Indeed, the influence of two of the variables appears to be greater on the former sort of perceived conflict than on the latter.

The import of these findings appears to be that the manner in which the leadership of an organization relates to rank-and-file members is not confined, in its effects, to social relations between the two strata. These effects filter down until they affect social relations among the lower-level members. In this way the personality characteristics of the leadership eventually leave their mark on the whole work milieu.

CHAPTER 8

Personal Predispositions

IN THE last few decades, psychologists have taken an increasing interest in the influence of personality upon cognitive functioning. An individual's perceptions, memories, and judgments are not simply a veridical mirror of reality. To some extent, they are also affected by his motives, his values, and other aspects of his personality.[1]

These considerations are germane here because the SF index, as we have seen, is largely perceptual in character. There is within each hotel variability among respondents on the SF index, so that even when the general environment is the same for all, respondents nevertheless vary in their scores on SF. Partially accounting for these individual variations are the personality tendencies of individual respondents. Solidary feelings are not only a product of environmental conditions such as the sympathy of management or the heterogeneity of members with respect to the Mach variable; they also seem to be related to the predispositions of the individual.

In demonstrating this with the data at hand, we shall set forth our findings with respect to each predisposition in two forms. First, we shall present tables showing the relationship between solidary feelings and a given personality tendency. Since, however, such a relationship could be spurious and due to the concentration of respondents with a certain personality characteristic in hotels with high or low organizational solidarity, we shall, in each instance, also present a second kind of table. In the latter, organizational solidarity will be controlled for while each predisposition is cross-tabulated with SF. This will enable us to see the relationship between a predisposition and solidary feelings when the "true," "objective" level of solidarity in the

1. Several studies illustrating this general proposition are: H. A. Murray, Jr., "The Effect of Fear Upon Estimates of the Maliciousness of Other Personalities," *Journal of Social Psychology*, 4 (1933):310–29; L. Postman, S. Bruner, and E. McGinnies, "Personal Values as Selective Factors in Perception," *Journal of Abnormal and Social Psychology*, 43 (1948):142–54; and C. W. Eriksen, "Some Implications for TAT Interpretations Arising from Need and Perception Experiments," *Journal of Personality*, 19 (1950): 282–88.

environment is held constant and will thus enable us in a rough manner to assess predispositional influences upon solidary feelings, independently of environmental influences.

Aggression

Contrary to our prediction, aggression on the part of top management was shown in the last chapter to be positively associated with solidary feelings among other employees. But what are the effects of a respondent's own level of aggression upon his SF score? Table 8.1 gives the cross-tabulation

TABLE 8.1
SF SCORES OF RESPONDENTS BY THEIR LEVEL OF AGGRESSION

	Aggression		
SF Scores	*Low*	*Medium*	*High*
Low	19%	26%	36%
Medium	36	39	36
High	45	35	27
	100	100	100
	(47)	(95)	(55)

$\chi^2 = 4.66$; df = 4; $.50 > p > .25$.

of the two variables. The figures disclose an inverse correlation: the greater a person's level of aggression, the less likely he is to have solidary feelings. Thus the effects of the respondent's aggression on SF is exactly opposite of the effects of management's aggression.

We are not certain how this paradox is to be explained. But perhaps we can obtain some clues from a study by M. Zuckerman.[2] A sample of sixty-three student nurses were asked in a mail questionnaire to nominate persons who best fitted certain behavioral descriptions from a list of names comprising the sample. One of the descriptive categories dealt with "hostile" persons, a second with persons "prejudiced" toward minorities. Four other behavioral traits for which nominations were made were "rebelliousness," "conformity," "submissiveness to authority," and "dependency." In order to qualify for a category, a person had to be nominated for it by at least two of her peers. Eight months prior to receiving the questionnaire, each subject had taken the Edwards Personal Preference Schedule.

The seven subjects who were described as "hostile" by their peers made the lowest mean score of all the groups on the need Aggression scale. That

2. See M. Zuckerman, "The Validity of the Edwards Personal Preference Schedule in the Measurement of Dependency-Rebelliousness," *Journal of Clinical Psychology*, 14 (1958): 379–82.

is to say, they scored lower on this scale than groups of "dependent," "submissive," and "conforming" students. This finding implies that the expression of hostility in their interpersonal relations is not a distinguishing characteristic of individuals who score high on the need Aggression scale of the EPPS, the scale from which the items for our own aggression index are taken.

What, then, does the scale measure? To score high, a person must endorse statements expressing strong feelings of anger—for example, "I *feel like* getting revenge," "I get so angry that I *feel like* throwing and breaking things." Zuckerman's finding that persons who are rated by their peers as hostile—that is, persons who presumably manifest hostility in their behavior—do not score high on the aggression scale therefore suggests that what the scale measures is the intensity of hostile affect, not the extent to which hostility is actually expressed in overt behavior. Apparently there is no one-to-one relationship between the two.[3]

This is not difficult to understand. Since the overt expression of hostility is, in general, subject to social disapproval, individuals who are prone to intense feelings of anger are likely to develop strong self-restraints when it comes to translating their affect into behavior. Or it may be that the causal relation operates in the other direction. Perhaps individuals who, for one reason or another, are inhibited about expressing anger are precisely the ones who build up hostile affect. Remaining pent up and unable to find an avenue of release, the feelings may come to possess extraordinary intensity.

Our line of reasoning here would explain why the inverse correlation which we predicted between the aggression of management and the solidary feelings of the rank and file does not show up in the data. Inasmuch as a high score on the aggression index does not necessarily signify a tendency to manifest hostility toward other personnel in the work milieu, an executive with high aggression would not be more likely than anyone else to provoke conflict and friction among employees. This interpretation, of course, explains only the absence of a negative correlation between the aggression of top management and the solidary feelings of the rank and file. Admittedly it does not explain why we obtain the positive correlation that we do.

A second finding of Zuckerman's sheds some light on the negative association we have found between the solidary feelings of respondents and their own aggression scores. Those student nurses who were characterized by their peers as being prejudiced toward ethnic minorities made the highest average score of all the groups on the need Aggression scale of EPPS.

3. This point receives empirical support from a study by Lesser. See G. S. Lesser, "The Relationship Between Overt and Fantasy Aggression as a Function of Maternal Response to Aggression," *Journal of Abnormal and Social Psychology*, 55 (1957):218–21.

It is permissible to equate prejudice here with making derogatory judgments of others. For one thing, prejudice by definition involves having unfavorable perceptions of the members of a minority group. A person who dislikes Negroes, for example, typically thinks of them as "dirty," "ignorant," "immoral," "lazy," and so forth. For another thing, there is empirical evidence for the tendency of prejudiced individuals to view other people in a disparaging way. The authors of *The Authoritarian Personality* found that, compared to the unprejudiced, prejudiced people are inclined toward a moralistic condemnation of others and toward blaming others.[4]

That the hostility of a person scoring high on the aggression index is not manifested in overt behavior does not mean that it is without effect on his psychological functioning. Insofar as these hostile feelings color social perceptions and give rise to derogatory judgments about others, it is not surprising that respondents who are high on the aggression index make comparatively low SF scores. For the SF index asks, among other things, about the respondent's perceptions of his fellow employees.

In this connection, it is instructive to examine the cross-tabulation of the aggression index with the items comprising the index of solidary feelings. Using the tau-beta coefficient to measure the strength of the correlation, we find that three of the four highest coefficients (those for items 1/72, 4/58, and 4/59) involve items explicitly voicing derogatory perceptions of the respondent's fellow employees.[5] Thus respondents with high aggression are relatively unlikely to consider employees "especially considerate" and are inclined to view both executive and nonexecutive personnel as deficient in loyalty to the hotel. By contrast, none of the four components of the SF index having low correlations directly express disparaging judgments of the individuals with whom a respondent works.[6] It seems, then, to be primarily those components of the SF index containing explicitly derogatory statements about fellow employees that account for the high correlation of SF with aggression.

To recapitulate our argument: the aggression index appears not to measure

4. See T. W. Adorno et al., *The Authoritarian Personality* (New York: Harper and Brothers, 1950), pp. 406–13.

5. The coefficient for the correlation of aggression with item 1/72 is .13; with item 4/58, −.13; with item 4/59, −.11.

6. One of these items refers to the amount of "mistrust" among personnel. Two others deal with the number of "quarrels and disputes" and with the degree of "tension and friction" during periods of heavy business. The fourth inquires how the respondent would feel if he had to leave his job at the hotel. Although these items can perhaps be construed as implying unfavorable perceptions of fellow employees, they differ from the three items with high correlations insofar as the latter are explicit. Most people, in our opinion, would agree that assertions that other employees are lacking in "consideration" and in "loyalty" to their employer, are disparaging.

the extent to which a person manifests hostility in overt behavior. Hence high scores of top management on the index do not result in low solidary feelings on the part of the rank and file. What the index does tap, in our opinion, is the intensity of hostile feelings, of the urge to direct hostility against others. These feelings color an individual's perceptions of other people and thereby affect his score on SF, so that aggression correlates negatively with solidary feelings.

What happens to the inverse correlation between aggression and solidary feelings when organizational solidarity is introduced as a third variable? The data reveal an interaction effect (table 8.2). If the organization has a

TABLE 8.2
THE PERCENTAGE OF RESPONDENTS HIGH ON THE SF INDEX BY THEIR LEVEL OF AGGRESSION AND BY ORGANIZATIONAL SOLIDARITY

Organizational Solidarity	*Aggression*	
	Low	*High*
Low	20% (49)	19% (43)
High	60% (53)	37% (52)

A vs. B: $\chi^2 = .19$; df = 1; $.75 > p > .50$. C vs. D: $\chi^2 = 4.57$; df = 1; $.05 > p > .025$. A vs. C: $\chi^2 = 14.6$; df = 1; $p < .005$. B vs. D: $\chi^2 = 2.51$; df = 1; $.25 > p > .10$.

high level of solidarity, the individual's predisposition seems to exercise a marked influence on his SF score. If, however, the level of solidarity in the environment is low, an individual's tendencies toward aggression have no effect on his SF score. So when environmental conditions discourage solidary feelings, the effects of the environment apparently blot out predispositional influences.

Another way to look at the table is to compare the rows. Such a comparison suggests that among people with high aggression, the environment has comparatively little effect on solidarity feelings, and that only among people with low aggression, does it have a great effect.

Abasement

A second predisposition that seems to affect solidary feelings is abasement (table 8.3). The figures indicate that the proportion high on solidary feelings varies directly with the level of abasement. People who direct their aggressions "inward" are relatively inclined to avoid derogatory thoughts about

TABLE 8.3
SF SCORES OF RESPONDENTS BY THEIR LEVEL OF ABASEMENT

SF Scores	*Abasement* Low	Medium	High
Low	33%	21%	26%
Medium	44	43	28
High	23	36	46
	100	100	100
	(78)	(42)	(78)

$\chi^2 = 10.382$; df = 4; $.05 > p > .025$.

fellow employees; they are less prone to see others as mistrustful, inconsiderate, lacking in loyalty, and engaged in conflict. This is conceivably the result of their tendency to blame themselves rather than others when things go wrong.

With the introduction of organizational solidarity as a control, a pattern similar to that for the aggression variable appears (table 8.4). The correlation

TABLE 8.4
PERCENTAGE OF RESPONDENTS HIGH ON THE SF INDEX BY THEIR LEVEL OF ABASEMENT AND BY ORGANIZATIONAL SOLIDARITY

Organizational Solidarity	*Abasement* Low	High
Low	12% (42)	26% (50)
High	33% (39)	57% (67)

A vs. B: $\chi^2 = 1.86$; df = 1; $.25 > p > .10$. C vs. D: $\chi^2 = 3.24$; df = 1; $.10 > p > .05$. A vs. C: $\chi^2 = 4.86$; df = 1; $.05 > p > .025$. B vs. D: $\chi^2 = 9.23$; df = 1; $p < .005$.

between abasement and solidary feelings still holds when environmental solidarity is held constant. But the influence of the predisposition is greater in hotels with a high level of organizational solidarity than in hotels with a low level of solidarity. Reading down each of the two columns of the table, moreover, we see that the environment has a greater effect among respondents who are high on abasement than among respondents who are low on abasement.

Machiavellianism

The last variable we have found to correlate with solidary feelings is Machiavellianism (table 8.5). The proportion high on SF varies inversely with

TABLE 8.5
SF SCORES OF RESPONDENTS BY THEIR MACHIAVELLIANISM

	Machiavellianism		
SF Scores	*Low*	*Medium*	*High*
Low	21%	25%	36%
Medium	32	40	39
High	47	34	25
	100	100	100
	(62)	(67)	(69)

$\chi^2 = 8.194$; df = 4; $.10 > p > .05$.

Machiavellianism, so that the higher a respondent's Mach score, the less likely he is to have solidary feelings. This finding should not surprise us in light of the Machiavellian's cynical and pessimistic view of other people. It is comprehensible that a person who, in general, is prone to believe that human beings are vicious and egoistic is likely, in any specific situation, to view his associates as inconsiderate and mistrustful, lacking in allegiance to collective interests, and given to friction with others.

Table 8.6 holds the environmental factor, organizational solidarity, constant. Again we find that the effects of the predispositional variable depend

TABLE 8.6
PERCENT OF RESPONDENTS HIGH ON THE SF INDEX BY MACHIAVELLIANISM AND BY ORGANIZATIONAL SOLIDARITY

	Machiavellianism	
Organizational Solidarity	*Low*	*High*
Low	17% (41)	22% (51)
High	62% (52)	35% (54)

A vs. B: $\chi^2 = .19$; df = 1; $.75 > p > .50$. C vs. D: $\chi^2 = 6.36$; df = 1; $.025 > p > .01$. A vs. C: $\chi^2 = 16.13$; df = 1; $p < .005$. B vs. D: $\chi^2 = 2.24$; df = 1; $.25 > p > .10$.

on the environment. In hotels with low organizational solidarity, there is little difference between Machiavellians and non-Machiavellians with respect to solidary feelings. In fact, somewhat more Machiavellians than non-Machiavellians make high SF scores. In hotels high on the collective measure of solidarity, on the other hand, the non-Machiavellians are much more likely to be high on SF. In short, the predisposition has a slight effect in one direction where the environment is adverse to solidarity but a marked effect in the opposite direction where the environment conduces to solidarity.

We obtain a somewhat different perspective on the table by reading down the columns. The figures tell us that among the Machiavellians, the environment accounts for relatively little variation in solidary feelings: Machiavellians are relatively low on SF regardless of the environment. The situation is strikingly different with the non-Machiavellians. Among them the environmental factor shows a strong correlation with SF. Machiavellians, then, have unsolidary feelings regardless of where they are, but whether the non-Machiavellians have solidary or unsolidary feelings depends on the environment.

Concluding Observations

Our findings concerning the effects of the three dispositional variables—aggression, abasement, and Machiavellianism—have one thing in common. If the environment is inimical to solidarity, predispositions have little effect on solidary feelings. It is as though the environmental forces overwhelmed predispositional influences. If, however, the environment is more favorable to solidarity, personality tendencies are given opportunity to operate and they exert considerable influence on solidary feelings.

An additional thread running through these three sets of findings, although not as clear-cut, is that those respondents whose scores on a given predisposition favor unsolidary feelings are less affected by environmental factors than those respondents whose scores favor solidary feelings. Thus respondents high on aggression are less affected than respondents low on aggression, respondents low on abasement less than respondents high on abasement, and respondents high on Machiavellianism less than respondents low on Machiavellianism.

Insofar as most of the items in the SF index are perceptual in character, inquiring about the respondent's perceptions of fellow employees or of the work milieu, the influence of predispositional variables upon solidary feelings may be understood as the result of distortions in the perception of an environment that is the same for everyone. Such an interpretation is, to be sure, plausible. Nonetheless, one can also argue that even though each hotel has a general atmosphere, which may affect all its employees, there are nuances in milieu and these nuances, to some extent, reflect the predispositions of the individuals involved. If a Machiavellian is more likely than a non-Machiavellian to perceive his fellow employees as mistrustful, it may be because he, by his own behavior, evokes mistrust in others. If an employee high on abasement says that he does not know of many quarrels among personnel, this may reflect the fact that he, being the kind that turns his hostilities "inward" on himself, does not elicit quarreling from others.

We are not arguing that this interpretation is necessarily superior to an interpretation in terms of perceptual distortion. If being high on aggression meant that a person had a propensity for becoming involved in conflict, we would expect high aggression on the part of management to be associated with low solidary feelings among rank-and-file employees. As we have seen, however, the findings are just the opposite. In the case of the other two predispositional factors, we do not have the means of testing which interpretation is closer to the facts. Nevertheless—and this is the point of these remarks—the argument for nuances in the environment as the intervening process merits serious consideration and therefore should not be ruled out. Hopefully, future research will provide a basis for choosing between the two alternative interpretations.

PART III
CONCLUSIONS

CHAPTER 9

Summary and Recommendations

A Résumé of the Findings

To RECAPITULATE the main findings of the study, we have seen that our data are largely, though not entirely, consistent with the Freudian theory of the superego. Freud argues that individuals acquire their moral code by identifying with their parents—i.e., internalizing the latter's standards. As predicted on the basis of Freudian theory, Machiavellianism shows correlations with the respondent's recollections of certain parental characteristics. Thus the greater the rapport the respondent had with his parents and the stricter they were, the less likely he is to be Machiavellian. Also, the more Machiavellian the respondent remembers his parents as having been, the more likely he is to be Machiavellian. Contrary to the intimations of Freudian theory, however, the punitiveness of the parents correlates positively with Machiavellianism.

Freudian theory also generates hypotheses relating a person's methods of handling aggression to Machiavellianism. These have been confirmed. The more a person directs his aggressive feelings outward onto other people, the higher his Mach score is. By contrast, abasement, the tendency to channel one's aggressive feelings onto oneself, is negatively associated with Machiavellianism. The findings with respect to aggression, however, are contrary to one of our predictions in that the methods of handling aggression do not mediate the effects of parental rapport upon Machiavellianism.

The writings of Charles H. Cooley have led us to examine the relationship of Machiavellianism to the looking-glass process. Here the data show that the greater a person's need for social approval and the greater his proclivity for "sympathizing" with others, the less inclined he is to be Machiavellian.

The orienting notion of solidarity, as derived from the works of Toennies and Sorokin, provide certain fruitful clues. Our most important finding here is that the urbanism of the locality the respondent resided in during adolescence correlates positively with Machiavellianism. This correlation, however, does not hold under all conditions. It is not found at all among respondents whose family milieus favored the development of a strong conscience. It is, on the other hand, strongest among respondents whose relations with their parents were highly conducive to Machiavellian attitudes. The urbanism of the locality currently resided in shows no relationship to Machiavellianism.

Our analysis of the work milieu in Part II is based on an index of solidary feelings. The personality composition of a hotel's employees seems to have a marked influence on SF scores. Three characteristics of hotels—a high level of Machiavellianism, an incongruity between the management and the rank and file in Mach scores, and heterogeneity among the rank and file with respect to Mach—are associated with low SF scores.

The personality characteristics of the management also affect the solidary feelings of employees. If managers are domineering, employees tend to have low SF scores. More interesting perhaps is the finding that hierarchical incongruity operates only in hotels whose managers are domineering. This is interpreted as indicating that where managers do not attempt to impose their values and their expectations on the rank and file, the existence of conflicting value orientations does not affect solidary feelings.

Sympathy and a high need for social approval among managers seem to have a salutary effect on the solidary feelings of rank-and-file employees. This effect, however, holds primarily in hotels in which the personality composition of employees is already conducive to solidary feelings.

Solidary feelings correlate with certain individual predispositions—positively with abasement and negatively with aggression and Machiavellianism. Such predispositions, however, operate only if the work milieu is solidary; in unsolidary milieus, they have practically no effect on SF scores.

Conclusions and Suggestions for Future Research

In an acute essay on the main theoretical problems in the field of personality and social structure, Alex Inkeles stresses the importance of examining the modal personality characteristics of the members of a social system or organization in order to understand role performance and organizational functioning. He writes:

> . . . role performance cannot safely be predicted solely on the basis of the extrinsic features of the status and its place in a larger social structure. The personalities of those occupying the statuses will strongly influence the quality of their role performance. And since it seems likely that personalities are not randomly recruited to statuses, the effects of modal personality patterns in any given group of status incumbents may be a massive influence on the quality

> of role performance in the group. The impact on other parts of the social structure may therefore be substantial.[1]

The cogency of Inkeles's thesis is underlined by our analysis of the personality composition of white-collar and managerial employees in hotels—an analysis that sought to order the data by relying heavily on role conflict as an unmeasured, intervening process.

Traditionally sociologists have viewed social structure as the source of role conflict. An example is provided by the proverbial situation in which the management expects the foreman to pressure the workers to increase productivity while the workers expect the foreman to go easy on them. The conflicting role expectations held by the management and by the rank-and-file employees are said to be an expression of their different positions in the organization.

Our analysis strongly suggests that a source of role conflict that has been neglected by sociologists is personality differences. Thus a cleavage between the average Machiavellian score of the top management and that of the rank and file (hierarchical incongruity) appears to foster role conflict, as does a large variation in Machiavellian scores among the rank and file (Machiavellian heterogeneity).

But to emphasize the personality sources of role conflict is not to belittle the significance of social structure. For incongruity between the management and the rank and file, as we saw, has a greater effect on solidary feelings than heterogeneity among the rank and file itself. This suggests that it is not role conflict between just any two segments of an organization that is important: we must know the positions held by the individuals holding conflicting expectations. A role conflict to which the top management is a party has more impact on organizational functioning than role conflict involving other members of the organization. This makes sense inasmuch as the top management has, on the average, more interaction than incumbents of any other position with all the various segments of the organization. It also makes sense because all other segments are expected to accept the guidance of the management, so that they have no choice but to cope, in one way or another, with the managers' expectations.

Modal personality characteristics do not affect only the existence or absence of role conflict. They also appear to have a bearing on its intensity. Where management scores high on an index of dominance, hierarchical incongruity has more impact on solidary feelings than where management scores low on dominance. Here, too, position in the organization is an

1. Alex Inkeles, "Personality and Social Structure," in R. K. Merton et al., eds., *Sociology Today: Problems and Prospects* (New York: Basic Books, 1959), pp. 266–67.

important variable. What counts is not the dominance of just any member of the organization—it is the dominance of the top management.

The interplay between personality and position is further brought out by our findings on sympathy and the need for social approval among the top management. These findings intimate that the personality characteristics of management affect its ability to meet the role expectations of other members of the organization. But here we meet with an even greater complexity in the data: these personality characteristics on the part of management have a salutary effect on the organizational functioning only where the organizational context is already favorable to the development of solidary feelings (e.g., under the conditions of low hierarchical incongruity).

Further studies exploring the interplay between personality composition and sociological variables in organizations are needed. Especially desirable would be replication to determine if our findings concerning the relation of the incongruity variables to solidary feelings hold up in other settings and with better measures of the dependent variable. Also, research should explore the relationship of incongruity to other dependent variables. Do members of groups with a high level of incongruity, for example, experience more psychological stress than members of groups with a low level?

Also important are the effects of varying levels of Machiavellianism in a group or organization. The maintenance of democracy in an organization would seem to depend, in part, on the willingness of members to abide by "the rules of the game." But it is doubtful that a Machiavellian atmosphere is conducive to respect for rules. Hence there is a question as to how successful Machiavellian organizations are in maintaining the essence, as opposed to the semblance, of democracy. Likewise, how do Machiavellian and non-Machiavellian groups compare on other variables? The psychological stress experienced by members might also be appropriate here.

The study of the modal level of Machiavellianism throws light on yet a further issue. Social control, we argued in the introduction, is often inoperative. In areas of social life in which this is so, the level of moral behavior is a function of the modal patterns of moral character. In our endeavor to understand these patterns, an analysis of the antecedents and correlates of the individual's score on Machiavellianism—such as Part I of this book presents—is an important step. But it is also essential for such understanding to ascertain whether different areas of social life vary in the average level of Machiavellianism. There is some evidence, for example, that relative to the members of other medical specialties, psychiatrists make the highest scores on the Mach scale.[2] If, as we suspect, there are variations in the

2. See R. Christie and F. Geis, "Some Consequences of Taking Machiavelli Seriously," in E. F. Borgatta & W. W. Lambert, eds., *Handbook of Personality Theory and Research* (Chicago: Rand McNally, 1968), pp. 964-65.

modal Mach scores, the question arises: what accounts for these variations? The nature of the work? The prestige and income attached to the work? The criteria and procedures used by gatekeepers in selecting new members of the occupation or the organization? By explaining modal differences in moral character, research would add to our understanding of one of the main sources of variation in the moral level of behavior.

The other main source of this variation is the effectiveness of social control mechanisms. Accounting for differences in effectiveness is a signal task facing sociologists. Earlier we suggested that modal Mach scores might be one antecedent of how effective social control is in an area of society. Other antecedents possibly worthwhile exploring are the prestige of an occupation, the setting in which the work is carried out (for example, large bureaucratic organizations vs. individual practice), and the power of the clientele and of other groups affected by the work.

The present study also suggests other problems that might be examined in future research.

1. In the first chapter, we cited one experiment showing the Machiavellians to be more "effective" than non-Machiavellians in a short-run situation in which the participants had not previously known each other. The experiment, however, leaves important questions unanswered. The term "effectiveness" does not convey a simple concept. To analyze it adequately, we have to specify the criteria for judging effectiveness and the individuals and groups who benefit from a given type of effectiveness. Moreover, we have to keep in mind that the personal qualities necessary for effectiveness will vary with the requirements of the situation or of the role.

In the study cited, the criterion of effectiveness was beating one's opponent in a competitive game, and the qualities necessary for success included the ability to persuade and manipulate others. How would the Machiavellian fare if the criteria and the situational requirements were different? What if success required the ability to bring out and foster the critical intelligence and creative independence of a group of children? What if the situation required not the brief interaction of an experiment but prolonged association—as, for example, in the relationship of a psychotherapist to his patient? Effectiveness is a legitimate and important subject for research, but this research must take considerations such as these into account.

2. We have shown that, as predicted, our measure of sympathy is negatively correlated with Mach. Several problems arise in this connection. The validity of our measure has not been conclusively demonstrated. Validating evidence beyond that which we have presented is called for. If our measure is not valid, there is a need to devise a valid measure which is not confounded with the person perception variable.

This is not to depreciate research on the latter variable. But the area of social perception strikes us as conceptually muddled insofar as there is no taxonomy of perception. We suspect that perceptual accuracy is not a unidimensional ability and that high and low scorers on the Mach scale will be found to be perceptually sensitive to different things. Machiavellians, for example, probably excel others in knowing who wields effective power in a group or organization. Non-Machiavellians, on the other hand, may be more appreciative of other people's feelings. In any event, a question worthy of study is how high and low scorers differ with respect to social perception.

3. If the measurement of sympathy has its problems, so does the measurement of solidarity. The measure of the latter concept that proved most fruitful for explaining the origins of Machiavellianism was the size of the community the respondent lived in as an adolescent. It would be desirable to ascertain if more refined measures of solidarity, such as the closeness of a person's ties to friends and relatives, relate to Machiavellianism. Although we have used such measures in the present research, these refer to social relations in adulthood. Our findings, however, suggest that the crucial period in the formation of a Machiavellian outlook comes before adulthood. If so, there is a need to use the more refined measures in a sample of adolescents or children.

Such a sample would also permit replication of our data about the individual's relations with his parents, employing indices in which we could have more confidence than those used here. Another advantage of studying young people is the opportunity it would provide for further exploring how the family milieu interacts with the social environment outside the home in influencing conscience.

4. As far as we know, the Mach scale has not yet been used in the study of out-and-out deviant individuals such as convicted criminals. Presumably certain classes of such deviants—for example, confidence men and extortionists—would tend to score high on Machiavellianism. This suggests an interesting problem: what are the differences between criminal Machiavellians and noncriminal Machiavellians? Are the differences primarily a matter of personality variables, such as intelligence or the ability to defer gratification? Or are the differences more a matter of social background, such as parental socioeconomic status or the relative availability of legitimate and illegitimate opportunity structures at a crucial stage of a person's development? [3]

3. The relevance of sociological factors to the origin of deviancy is discussed in R. K. Merton, *Social Theory and Social Structure* (Glencoe, Ill.: Free Press, 1957), chaps. 4 and 5; and R. A. Cloward, "Illegitimate Means, Anomie, and Deviant Behavior," *American Sociological Review*, 24 (1959):164–76.

It is difficult to say if the moral level of North America in the middle of the twentieth century is lower than that of other societies, past and present. Nonetheless, there is much truth, in our judgment, to the assertions of social scientists such as Pitirim A. Sorokin, C. Wright Mills, and Edgar Z. Friedenberg that our society is shot through with moral corruption. Writing of the growing signs of alienation among our nation's youth, Friedenberg puts the matter aptly:

> Our concern about the young is . . . valid, but there is a note of panic in it stemming from our own guilt. When we ask, "What is disturbing them?", we mean also, "How much do they know about what is really going on, and will they buy it?" When we ask, "Are their protest movements Communist-dominated?", we are also asking, "Can they really be convinced without having been tricked or misled, that our way of life has become viciously irresponsible and destructive? Is it, after all, so obvious that even the young can notice it for themselves?"[4]

If these questions are valid, it is incumbent upon scholars to apply their sociological imaginations to enlarging our empirical knowledge of morality. The problems outlined above perhaps provide as good a point of departure as any for such a quest.

4. Edgar Z. Friedenberg, "A Polite Encounter Between the Generations," *New York Times Magazine*, January 16, 1966, p. 73.

APPENDIX

Indices of the Study

This Appendix describes each index employed in the study, listing the items comprising the index and giving the marginals for it. Each item is designated by the deck and the left-most column number of the field in which it is punched in the data decks. The figures in parentheses in the marginals denote the limits of each category.

For convenience of organization, the indices are grouped into four sections: (1) those having to do with the respondent's youth, (2) those measuring personality characteristics, (3) those pertaining to each respondent's current interpersonal and social relations, and (4) collective variables describing the work milieu.

Indices Pertaining to Youth

PERCEIVED MACHIAVELLIANISM OF PARENTS

As in the case of the other parent variables, three separate indices have been calculated for this variable: the perceived Machiavellianism of (1) the respondent's father, (2) the respondent's mother, and (3) the parent of the same sex as the respondent. These indices are based on four items each. The responses to each item have been divided into four categories; responses in the most Machiavellian direction have been assigned a value of three, those in the least Machiavellian direction a value of zero, and those in between values of one or two. If a respondent makes no reply to any of the four items or if the four items do not apply to him (e.g., there was no father figure in the household in which he lived during his adolescence), he is not scored on the index. A person's score on each index is derived by summing his scores on the four items. The theoretical range is zero to twelve. Here are the four items comprising each index:

> Below are two statements. . . . Please indicate the extent to which your parents each would agree or disagree with them by placing a check mark

in the appropriate space. (If one or both of your parents are dead, indicate what their opinion would have been when they were living.)

1/67 1/68 "It is safest to assume that all people have a vicious streak and it will come out when they are given a chance." [Possible responses range from "strongly agree" to "strongly disagree" for each parent.]

1/69 1/70 "There is no excuse for lying to someone else." [Possible replies vary from "strongly agree" to "strongly disagree" for each parent.]

Below is a series of phrases. We want to know *how accurately* each phrase describes each of your *parents* during the period when you were in your teens . . . .

3/68 3/69 Was unsuspicious and trustful toward people. [Each respondent has five replies from which to choose. These range from "highly true" to "highly false" for each parent.]

3/74 3/75 Was willing to engage in deception when there was good reason to do so. [Possible replies vary from "highly true" to "highly false" for each parent.]

The following are the marginals on a trichotomized version of each of the indices:

Perceived Mach of Father	
Low (0–3)	156
Medium (4–5)	119
High (6–12)	149
Not scored	59
	483

Perceived Mach of Mother	
Low (0–3)	173
Medium (4–5)	123
High (6–12)	158
Not scored	29
	483

Perceived Mach of Same-Sex Parent	
Low (0–2)	96
Medium (3–5)	177
High (6–12)	158
Not scored	52
	483

PERCEIVED RAPPORT WITH PARENTS

Three indices have been calculated for this variable: perceived rapport with (1) the respondent's father, (2) the respondent's mother, and (3) the parent of the same sex as the respondent. Each index is based on three items. We have trichotomized the responses to each item, assigning values of zero, one, or two for each response. If any of the items does not apply or if there is no answer to any of them, the respondent is not given a score on the index. The theoretical range is from zero to six. The items for this variable are listed below:

3/61 3/62 When you were a teenager, did your parents participate in recreational activities with you, such as going on picnics with you, playing games with you, going to athletic events with you, etc.? . . . If yes for either or both parents, how often did he (she) do such things with you? [Possible replies range from "no" to "very often" for each parent.]

3/64 3/65 As a teenager, did you confide in your parents and tell them your troubles? . . . If yes for either or both parents, how often did you confide in him (her)? [Possible responses range from "no" to "very often" for each parent.]

4/12 4/13 Below is a series of phrases. We want to know *how accurately* each phrase describes each of your *parents* during the period *when you were in your teens*. . . . Was very effective in helping his (her) children through the various emotional crises usually associated with growing up. [Possible replies range from "highly true" to "highly false."]

The marginals for the three indices follow:

Perceived Rapport with Father	
Low (0–2)	194
Medium (3–4)	121
High (5–6)	104
Not scored	64
	483

Perceived Rapport with Mother	
Low (0–3)	214
Medium (4–5)	152
High (6)	93
Not scored	24
	483

Perceived Rapport with Same-Sex Parent	
Low (0–1)	108
Medium (2–4)	188
High (5–6)	136
Not scored	51
	483

PERCEIVED PUNITIVENESS OF PARENTS

Two items comprise each of the indices for this variable. Each item has been given code values of zero to three, depending on whether the response was in the punitive or nonpunitive direction. Respondents to whom either of the items does not apply or who give no reply to either of the items have been left out of the scoring. The scores can range from zero to six. The following are the index items:

3/54 3/55 How often were you spanked or given other physical punishment *as a child* . . . by your father . . . by your mother? [Possible replies vary from "almost every day" to "never."]

4/6 4/7 We want to know *how accurately* each phrase describes each of your *parents* during the period *when you were in your teens*. . . . Tried to reason with his (her) children when they misbehaved, rather than using some form of punishment. [Possible responses range from "highly true" to "highly false."]

Respondents are distributed as follows on the three indices:

Perceived Punitiveness of Father	
Low (0–1)	152
Medium (2–3)	154
High (4–6)	116
Not scored	61
	483

Perceived Punitiveness of Mother	
Low (0)	85
Medium (1–3)	257
High (4–6)	119
Not scored	22
	483

Perceived Punitiveness of Same-Sex Parent	
Low (0–1)	141
Medium (2–3)	171
High (4–6)	123
Not scored	48
	483

PERCEIVED STRICTNESS OF PARENTS

The two items making up each of the indices of this variable have been assigned code values of zero, one, or two. A "no answer" or "does not apply" to either of the items results in the index being unscored. Scores can vary from zero to six. The two items read as follows:

3/70 3/71 We want to know *how accurately* each phrase describes each of your *parents* during the period *when you were in your teens.* . . . Was strict toward his (her) children. [Possible replies vary from "highly true" to "highly false."]

4/10 4/11 We want to know *how accurately* each phrase describes each of your *parents* during the period *when you were in your teens.* . . . Was "soft" with regard to disciplining his (her) children. [The respondent is asked to check one of five possible replies, which vary from "highly true" to "highly false."]

The marginals for the three indices are given below:

Perceived Strictness of Father	
Low (0–1)	159
Medium (2)	115
High (3–4)	152
Not scored	57
	483

Perceived Strictness of Mother	
Low (0–1)	195
Medium (2)	124
High (3–4)	142
Not scored	22
	483

Perceived Strictness of Same-Sex Parent	
Low (0–1)	153
Medium (2)	123
High (3–4)	139
Not scored	68
	483

COMPOSITE INDEX OF PARENT VARIABLES

This index is derived by aggregating the scores on four variables, all referring to characteristics of the same-sex parent. These are: (1) punitiveness, (2) rapport, (3) strictness, and (4) perceived Machiavellianism. We have dichotomized each component, assigning a value of one to respondents scoring in the Machiavellian direction and a value of zero to respondents scoring in the opposite direction. In each case, about a third of the respondents receive a value of one and about two-thirds a value of zero. The points a respondent receives on the components are summed to arrive at his score on the composite index. Thus a high score on the index indicates a family milieu relatively favorable to the development of Machiavellianism; a low score, a milieu relatively unfavorable. The theoretical range for the index is zero to four. Respondents who received no score on any of the components are not scored on the composite index.

The following is the frequency distribution of respondents on a four-category version of the index.

Low (0)	92
Medium-Low (1)	123
Medium-High (2)	112
High (3–4)	69
Not scored	87
	483

PERCEIVED RAPPORT WITH SCHOOL AUTHORITIES

Responses to each of the two items comprising this index have been trichotomized and given codes of zero, one, or two. A "no answer" or "does not apply" for either item results in the case being left out of the analysis. The theoretical range is zero to four. The items follow:

1/74 How true is each statement? . . . When I was a teenager, I didn't care much for school. [The respondent can select one of four replies, which vary from "highly true" to "highly false."]

3/26 What did most of your teachers think of you as a teenager? [Possible replies range from "they thought very highly of you" to "they had a strong dislike for you."]

The marginals for this index are as follows:

Low (0)	93
Medium (1–2)	204
High (3–4)	167
Not scored	19
	483

Measures of Personality

MACHIAVELLIANISM

The twelve items for this index are adapted from a forced-choice scale developed by Richard Christie. Each item consists of a pair of statements.

One is keyed to the Mach variable; the other is equivalent to the keyed statement in social desirability but is not related to Machiavellianism. The respondent is asked to indicate which of the two statements he prefers or with which he is in greater agreement. Each item is scored two for a Machiavellian response, zero for a non-Machiavellian response, and one for no answer. If a respondent fails to reply to more than four items, he is given no score on the variable. Index scores range from zero to twenty-four.

Below are listed the items of the index. An asterisk indicates which statement in each pair is keyed to the Mach variable. A keyed statement, however, does not necessarily represent a Machiavellian response (i.e., checking it does not necessarily give the respondent two points). It does so only when it is worded in the "original" direction—i.e., when the statement, as phrased, conveys a Machiavellian attitude. An example of such a statement is, "Never tell anyone the real reason you did something unless it is useful to do so." When the wording of the keyed statement is "reversed," it indicates a non-Machiavellian attitude, and the respondent therefore receives a score of zero for checking it in preference to the other statement of the pair. In such a case, a score of two can be obtained only by endorsement of the non-keyed statement. An example of a reversed statement is, "Honesty is the best policy in all cases."

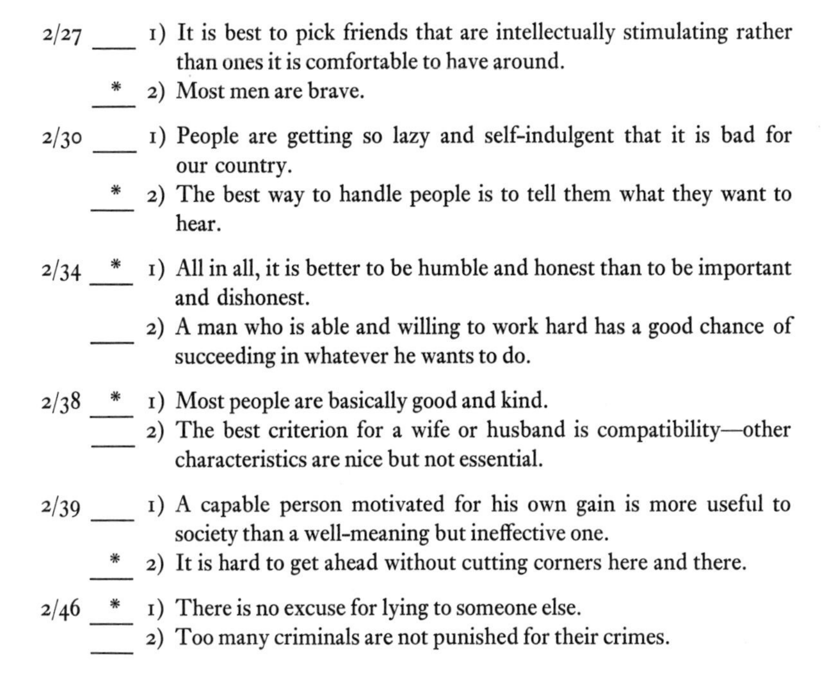

2/27 ___ 1) It is best to pick friends that are intellectually stimulating rather than ones it is comfortable to have around.
_*_ 2) Most men are brave.

2/30 ___ 1) People are getting so lazy and self-indulgent that it is bad for our country.
_*_ 2) The best way to handle people is to tell them what they want to hear.

2/34 _*_ 1) All in all, it is better to be humble and honest than to be important and dishonest.
___ 2) A man who is able and willing to work hard has a good chance of succeeding in whatever he wants to do.

2/38 _*_ 1) Most people are basically good and kind.
___ 2) The best criterion for a wife or husband is compatibility—other characteristics are nice but not essential.

2/39 ___ 1) A capable person motivated for his own gain is more useful to society than a well-meaning but ineffective one.
_*_ 2) It is hard to get ahead without cutting corners here and there.

2/46 _*_ 1) There is no excuse for lying to someone else.
___ 2) Too many criminals are not punished for their crimes.

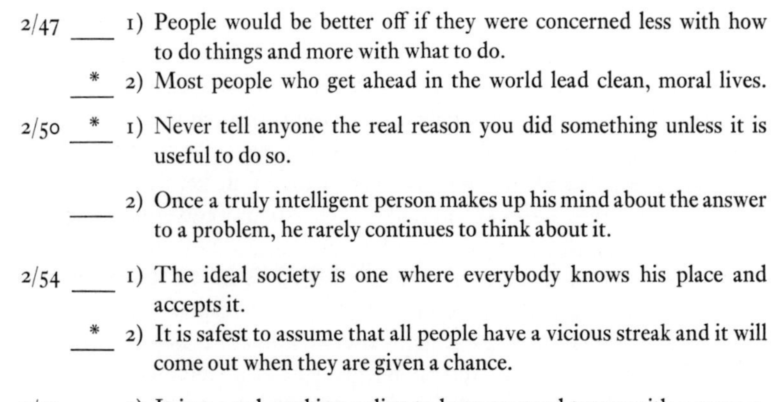

2/47 ___ 1) People would be better off if they were concerned less with how to do things and more with what to do.

* 2) Most people who get ahead in the world lead clean, moral lives.

2/50 * 1) Never tell anyone the real reason you did something unless it is useful to do so.

___ 2) Once a truly intelligent person makes up his mind about the answer to a problem, he rarely continues to think about it.

2/54 ___ 1) The ideal society is one where everybody knows his place and accepts it.

* 2) It is safest to assume that all people have a vicious streak and it will come out when they are given a chance.

2/55 ___ 1) It is a good working policy to keep on good terms with everyone.

* 2) Honesty is the best policy in all cases.

2/61 * 1) It is wise to flatter important people.

___ 2) Once a decision has been made, it is best to keep changing it as new circumstances arise.

2/62 ___ 1) Once a way of handling problems has been worked out, it is best to stick with it.

* 2) One should take action only when sure that it is morally right.

Respondents are distributed as follows on a trichotomized version of the index.

Low (0–8)	164
Medium (9–13)	167
High (14–24)	150
Not scored	2
	483

THE NEED FOR SOCIAL APPROVAL

The ten items making up this index have been taken from the Lykken Anxiety Scale. Each item consists of a description of two activities or events, the respondent being required to choose which of the two he would prefer. If, in replying to an item, he checks the statement keyed to the variable, he is given no points; if he checks the other statement, he is given two points; if he gives no reply at all, he receives one point. When there are no answers to three or more items, the respondent is not included in the analysis. The score can vary from zero to twenty.

In the following list of index items, the keyed activity is indicated by an asterisk.

2/15 _*_ 1) Your dog tears up the neighbor's newspaper and you have to go over and apologize.
___ 2) Addressing fifty Christmas cards.

2/16 ___ 1) Cleaning up a spilled bottle of syrup.
_*_ 2) Mistakenly saying "hello" to someone you didn't know.

2/17 _*_ 1) Being cursed by an old friend.
___ 2) Waiting in line for two hours to pay a parking ticket.

2/18 ___ 1) Spending an evening with some boring people.
_*_ 2) You lose your bus fare and can't pay.

2/19 _*_ 1) Joking about how homely Mary is and hearing Mary's voice behind you say: "I heard that."
___ 2) Having your empty car smashed.

2/20 ___ 1) Have to bathe in cold water because the water heater is broken.
_*_ 2) Ask a friend for a loan and be refused.

2/21 _*_ 1) Someone says loudly to you at a party: "Why don't you go home? Nobody wants you here."
___ 2) Cleaning out a cesspool.

2/22 ___ 1) Waiting for an overdue bus.
_*_ 2) Having to ask the person behind you at a movie to stop kicking your seat.

2/23 ___ 1) Carrying a ton of coal from the backyard into the basement.
_*_ 2) Walking into a room full of people, you stumble on a footstool and sprawl on the floor.

2/24 _*_ 1) Having to tell somebody you know they're lying.
___ 2) Digging a big rubbish pit.

The marginals for this index are as follows:

Low (0–7)	153
Medium (8–11)	175
High (12–20)	153
Not scored	2
	483

SYMPATHY

Seven items, taken from the need Intraception scale of the Edwards Personal Preference Schedule, constitute this index. An item is given two points if the response indicates high sympathy; no points if it indicates low sympathy; and one point if there is no answer. A case is left unscored on the variable if there are no answers to more than two items. The scores can theoretically vary from zero to fourteen.

The items are in forced-choice format, the respondent having to choose between the two statements given in each item. Keyed statements are indicated by an asterisk in the list of items that follow.

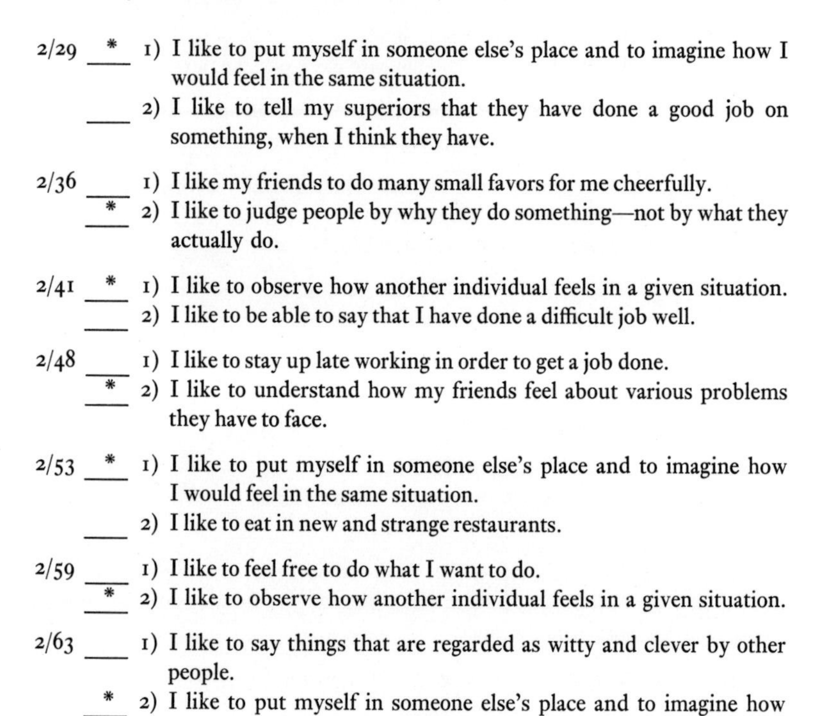

2/29 _*_ 1) I like to put myself in someone else's place and to imagine how I would feel in the same situation.
___ 2) I like to tell my superiors that they have done a good job on something, when I think they have.

2/36 ___ 1) I like my friends to do many small favors for me cheerfully.
_*_ 2) I like to judge people by why they do something—not by what they actually do.

2/41 _*_ 1) I like to observe how another individual feels in a given situation.
___ 2) I like to be able to say that I have done a difficult job well.

2/48 ___ 1) I like to stay up late working in order to get a job done.
_*_ 2) I like to understand how my friends feel about various problems they have to face.

2/53 _*_ 1) I like to put myself in someone else's place and to imagine how I would feel in the same situation.
___ 2) I like to eat in new and strange restaurants.

2/59 ___ 1) I like to feel free to do what I want to do.
_*_ 2) I like to observe how another individual feels in a given situation.

2/63 ___ 1) I like to say things that are regarded as witty and clever by other people.
_*_ 2) I like to put myself in someone else's place and to imagine how I would feel in the same situation.

The marginals for a three-category version of this variable are as follows:

Low (0–5)	135
Medium (6–9)	199
High (10–14)	147
Not scored	2
	483

THE LOOKING-GLASS PROCESS

This index is based on the two previous variables—sympathy and the need for social approval. Each respondent's score is calculated by summing his scores on the two components. To give the two components equal ranges we have multiplied each by a correction factor before summing. Since the range for the sympathy index is 0 to 14, it is multiplied by ten. The index of the need for social approval, having a range of 0 to 20, is multiplied by seven. Thus the two components each have a theoretical range of 0 to 140 and the index as a whole has a theoretical range of 0 to 280.

If a respondent is given no score on either of the constituent indices because of a large number of "no answers," he is not assigned a score on the composite index.

The marginals are as follows:

Low (0–99)	111
Medium-Low (100–129)	115
Medium-High (130–169)	123
High (170–280)	130
Not scored	4
	483

AGGRESSION

This index consists of six forced-choice items taken from the need Aggression scale of the Edwards Personal Preference Schedule. For each item, a respondent is given two points for a response indicating high aggression; no points for a response indicating low aggression; and one point if he fails to reply to the item. A respondent is not scored if he has more than two "no answers."

The following are the constituent items of the index, with asterisks showing keyed statements.

2/25 _*_ 1) I feel like telling other people off when I disagree with them.
___ 2) I like to participate in new fads and fashions.

2/32 ___ 1) I like to listen to or to tell jokes in which sex plays a major part.
_*_ 2) I feel like getting revenge when someone has insulted me.

2/43 ___ 1) I like to have my life so arranged that it runs smoothly and without change in my plans.
_*_ 2) I get so angry that I feel like throwing and breaking things.

2/49 ___ 1) I like my friends to confide in me and to tell me their troubles.
_*_ 2) I like to attack points of view that are contrary to mine.

2/56 _*_ 1) I feel like blaming others when things go wrong for me.
___ 2) I like to ask questions which I know no one will be able to answer.

2/60 _*_ 1) I feel like getting revenge when someone has insulted me.
___ 2) When I am in a group, I like to accept the leadership of someone else in deciding what the group is going to do.

The marginals for the aggression index follow:

Low (0–3)	129
Medium (4–6)	212
High (7–12)	138
Not scored	4
	483

ABASEMENT

The six forced-choice items comprising this index come from the need Abasement scale of the Edwards Personal Preference Schedule. Two points are given for a high response, no points for a low response, and one point for no answer. No score is assigned to those respondents who fail to reply to more than two items in the index. The theoretical range is from zero to twelve. An asterisk denotes the keyed statement in each item.

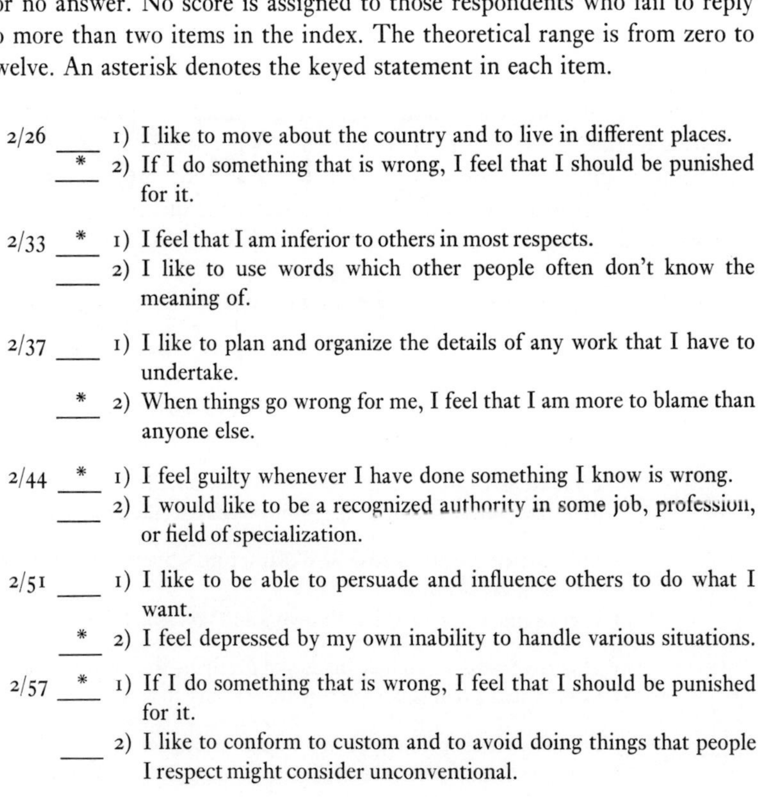

2/26 ___ 1) I like to move about the country and to live in different places.
_*_ 2) If I do something that is wrong, I feel that I should be punished for it.

2/33 _*_ 1) I feel that I am inferior to others in most respects.
___ 2) I like to use words which other people often don't know the meaning of.

2/37 ___ 1) I like to plan and organize the details of any work that I have to undertake.
_*_ 2) When things go wrong for me, I feel that I am more to blame than anyone else.

2/44 _*_ 1) I feel guilty whenever I have done something I know is wrong.
___ 2) I would like to be a recognized authority in some job, profession, or field of specialization.

2/51 ___ 1) I like to be able to persuade and influence others to do what I want.
_*_ 2) I feel depressed by my own inability to handle various situations.

2/57 _*_ 1) If I do something that is wrong, I feel that I should be punished for it.
___ 2) I like to conform to custom and to avoid doing things that people I respect might consider unconventional.

Respondents are distributed on the index in the following manner:

Low (0–4)	180
Medium (5–7)	115
High (8–12)	187
Not scored	1
	483

THE BALANCE BETWEEN AGGRESSION AND ABASEMENT

Each respondent's score on this index is calculated by subtracting his score on the abasement index from his score on the aggression index. Scores can theoretically range from -12 to 12. The distribution of the respondents on a trichotomized version of the index is as follows:

Abasiveness predominant (-12 to -3)	151
Neither predominant (-2 to $+1$)	181
Aggression predominant ($+2$ to $+12$)	147
Not scored	4
	483

Indices of Interpersonal and Social Relations

FREQUENCY OF SEEING FRIENDS AND ACQUAINTANCES

This index is based on three items. Each item has been assigned code values of one to seven. If the respondent gives no answer to any of the three items, he is left out of the scoring. The scores can range from three to twenty-one. The component items read:

1/43 Within the *last six months*, have you gotten together socially with any of the neighbors on your block (*not* including relatives)? . . . How often, in general, do you get together socially with neighbors on your block? [Possible replies vary from "less often than once a year" to "a few times a week (or more often)."]

1/47 Within the *last six months*, have you gotten together socially, *outside of working hours*, with any of the people you know at work (*not* including relatives or neighbors)? . . . How often, in general, do you get together socially with people you know at work (*outside of working hours*)? [Possible replies vary from "less often than once a year" to "a few times a week (or more often)."]

1/51 Within the *last six months*, have you gotten together socially with any friends or acquaintances *other than* relatives, neighbors on your block or people you know at work? . . . How often, in general, do you get together socially with friends or acquaintances? [Possible replies vary from "less often than once a year" to "a few times a week (or more often)."]

The frequency distribution for a four-category version of the variable is as follows:

Low (3–6)	120
Medium-Low (7–8)	109
Medium-High (9–11)	148
High (12–21)	103
Not scored	3
	483

INTIMACY OF FRIENDSHIP TIES

Six items comprise this index. Each component is assigned code values of zero to three. A "no answer" to any constituent item results in the respondent being left out of the analysis. The theoretical range is from zero to eighteen.

The respondent gives five responses to each of the items below, one for each of "the *five persons* (or married couples) *not related* to you, *whom you know best*." The scoring of the first four items is based on the number of friends to whom, according to the respondent, a given statement applies.

2/66 You would feel badly if you happened to lose touch with this person.

2/67 You know the immediate family of this person well.

2/68 This person has given you a gift within the past 12 months (for your birthday, for Christmas, etc.)

2/69 The two closest friends of this person (not including yourself) are good friends of yours.

2/70 Write in the number of years you have known each person. [This item is used to compute the mean percent of the respondent's life that he has known the five friends listed. This proportion determines the score assigned to each respondent.]

3/08 How about the *number of different kinds* of things you talk about with each of the above persons? *Write in the letters* designating those with whom you discuss:

One or two subjects of mutual interest ________________

Several subjects of mutual interest ________________

Quite a few subjects of mutual interest ________________

A very wide range of subjects of mutual interest ________________

[The first alternative is given a score of one, the last a score of four, and those in between scores of two and three. The respondent receives a score for each friend, and the scores for the five friends are then summed to yield a total score for the item. The latter score determines the code value assigned for this item.]

The frequency distribution of respondents on this index is as follows:

Low (0–5)	112
Medium-Low (6–9)	115
Medium-High (10–12)	106
High (13–18)	129
Not scored	21
	483

CLOSENESS OF TIES WITH KIN

This index consists of four items, each of which includes a list of categories of relatives. In replying, the respondent indicates to which, if any, of the categories the item applies. On the basis of the number of categories checked, the respondent receives zero, one, or two points for the item. Respondents who fail to reply to any component are not scored at all. The theoretical range is zero to eight. The component items are as follows:

1/60 *Within the last six months*, have you asked for advice about a personal matter from any relative outside of your own household? . . . *If yes*, from which of the following have you asked such advice within the last six months? (Check one or more.)

1/62 *Within the last 12 months* have any relatives outside of your own household given you a gift (such as for your birthday, at Christmas time, etc.)? . . . *If yes*, which of the following have given you a gift within the last 12 months? (Check one or more.)

1/64 Are there any relatives outside of your own household with whom you have lively discussions about those things that interest you most? . . . *If yes*, with which of the following do you have such discussions? (Check one or more.)

1/66 *Within the last six months*, have you (or your family) loaned something to, or borrowed something from, any relative outside your own household? . . . *If yes*, with which of the following have you loaned or borrowed something within the last six months? (Check one or more.)

The frequency distribution for the four-category version of the index is as follows:

Low (0–1)	132
Medium-Low (2–3)	150
Medium-High (4–5)	109
High (6–8)	88
Not scored	4
	483

SOLIDARY FEELINGS

The SF index consists of eight items. We have trichotomized each item, giving respondents two points for a response in the highly solidary direction, one point for a medium response, and no points for a low response. Respondents' scores for the eight items have been summed to yield an index with a range of zero to sixteen. The following are the items comprising the index:

1/72 How true is each statement? . . . Most people at my place of work seem to be especially considerate of others.

1/75 How true is each statement? . . . The people at my place of work tend to distrust each other.

4/38 How accurately does each of the sentences below describe *the particular work you are presently doing*? . . . During periods of heavy business, there is tension and friction among the employees with whom you work.

4/45 *Within the past three weeks*, how many separate disputes or quarrels have you heard of or personally witnessed?

a) between *managerial* and *non-managerial* employees? (Write in the number) . . .

b) among *managerial* employees? . . .

c) among *non-managerial* employees? . . .

[The scoring of this item is based on the sum of disputes and quarrels given in response to the three parts of the item.]

4/51 Say circumstances compelled you to leave your job at this hotel and take *similar work* with *similar pay* elsewhere. How would you feel about leaving? [Possible responses range from "very glad" to "very badly."]

4/57 Which of the following phrases best characterizes the relations between management and the rest of the employees here? [Possible responses vary from "fairly hostile" to "very friendly."]

4/58 Judging from the people with whom you have contact, how much loyalty to the hotel is there . . . among executive employees?

4/59 Judging from the people with whom you have contact, how much loyalty to the hotel is there . . . among non-executive employees?

Respondents from hotels included in those chapters of the study dealing with solidarity in the work environment distributed themselves as follows on the index:

Low (0–6)	55
Medium (7–10)	74
High (11–16)	69
Not scored	7
	205

Respondents who give no reply to one or more items in the index are not scored.

Collective Measures of the Work Milieu

The measures below refer to properties of the hotel environment or to the characteristics of top management in each hotel. Certain points should be noted about these collective variables. First, in calculating index scores, a value of one has been added to the score of each individual whose score is used in computing the index. When we compute the standard deviation of Mach scores among the rank-and-file employees of a hotel, for example, one is added to the Mach score of each respondent before the calculations are performed. This is necessary because of the mechanics of the cross-tabulation program of the Bureau of Applied Social Research at Columbia University, on which the calculations have been performed. In no way, however, does this procedure alter the rank order of hotels on each variable. Therefore it does not affect our findings at all. Second, the frequency distributions given for these variables are based only on those respondents and hotels that are included in our analysis of solidary feelings and organizational solidarity. The others are excluded from the base figures. Finally, some of the organizational variables measure the characteristics of the "top management" in each hotel. This group, by definition, includes the general manager and that executive who is second in command and shares in the over-all direction of the hotel's activities. When a hotel lacks the latter type of official, only the general manager is meant.

ORGANIZATIONAL SOLIDARITY

This is a collective variable intended to characterize the work environment. It is the mean score on the SF index of all respondents from each hotel. The frequency distribution of hotels and of respondents on the four-category version of this variable is as follows:

	Hotels	Respondents
Low (4.63–8.39)	5	56
Medium-Low (8.55–9.09)	4	40
Medium-High (9.77–10.13)	4	50
High (10.50–13.67)	8	59
	21	205

MACHIAVELLIAN LEVEL OF THE HOTEL

This is a collective variable designed to measure how Machiavellian the respondents from a hotel are. It is operationally defined as the mean Mach score of all the respondents in a hotel. The following are the marginals for this variable:

	Hotels	Respondents
Low (9.50–11.20)	6	61
Medium (11.31–12.67)	6	71
High (13.09–15.00)	9	73
	21	205

HIERARCHICAL INCONGRUITY

This variable is intended to tap the degree of incongruity in Mach scores between the top management and rank-and-file respondents (all those outside of top management). It is defined as the mean Mach score of top management minus the mean Mach score of the rank and file. The marginals for it are:

	Hotels	Respondents
Rank and File Higher (−8.33 to −3.43)	9	96
Small Difference (−.67 to +.67)	5	44
Management Higher (2.00 to 6.50)	7	65
	21	205

One aspect of the variable deserves some explanation. The frequency distribution of respondents and hotels on hierarchical incongruity shows a marked skewness. The proportion of cases in the "small difference" category is relatively small, that in the category "rank and file higher" relatively large. The reason for locating the cutting points that separate the three categories where we have is that there are "natural" gaps at these points. The scores in the "small difference" category have a range of only 1.00. By contrast, the hotels with the lowest degree of incongruity in each of the two "large difference" categories differ from the closest scoring hotels in the "small difference" category by 2.76 points and 1.33 points, respectively. Thus the gaps separating the "small difference" category from the other two categories are each larger than the range of the "small difference" category itself. If we have sacrificed symmetry of distribution, we have done so in order to avoid arbitrary cutting points for the categories.

HETEROGENEITY OF MACHIAVELLIANISM

This is defined as the standard deviation of Mach scores among rank-and-file respondents in a hotel. Marginals for a trichotomized version of the variable are as follows:

	Hotels	*Respondents*
Low (1.15–3.85)	9	83
Medium (4.06–4.24)	5	56
High (4.80–6.39)	7	66
	21	205

THE MACHIAVELLIANISM OF TOP MANAGEMENT

This is the mean Mach score of the top management. The frequency distribution is as follows:

	Hotels	*Respondents*
Low (3–8)	6	74
Medium (10–13)	8	69
High (13.5–18)	7	62
	21	205

THE DOMINANCE OF TOP MANAGEMENT

Our index of dominance consists of six items taken from the need Dominance scale of the Edwards Personal Preference Schedule. The items are in forced-choice format, the respondent being asked to indicate which of the two statements in each item is more descriptive of himself. Each item is coded two for a high response, zero for a low response, and one for a no answer. If more than two items receive no reply, the respondent is not given a score. The theoretical range is from zero to twelve.

The following are the items constituting the index. The statement in each item keyed to the dominance variable is indicated by an asterisk.

2/28 ___ 1) When I am in a group, I like to accept the leadership of someone else in deciding what the group is going to do.

* ___ 2) I like to supervise and to direct the actions of other people whenever I can.

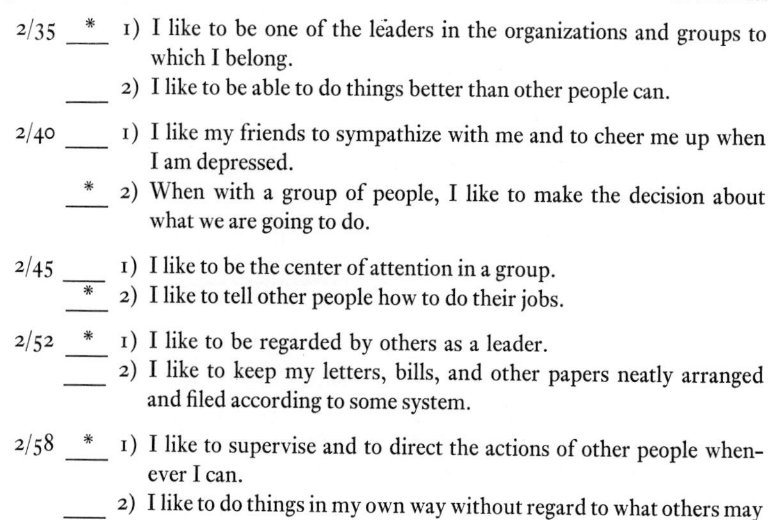

2/35 * 1) I like to be one of the leaders in the organizations and groups to which I belong.

2) I like to be able to do things better than other people can.

2/40 1) I like my friends to sympathize with me and to cheer me up when I am depressed.

* 2) When with a group of people, I like to make the decision about what we are going to do.

2/45 1) I like to be the center of attention in a group.

* 2) I like to tell other people how to do their jobs.

2/52 * 1) I like to be regarded by others as a leader.

2) I like to keep my letters, bills, and other papers neatly arranged and filed according to some system.

2/58 * 1) I like to supervise and to direct the actions of other people whenever I can.

2) I like to do things in my own way without regard to what others may think.

The dominance of top management is the mean score of the two leading executives in each hotel on the dominance index. This variable is a collective variable, referring to the property of a hotel. The frequency distribution of hotels and of respondents on a three-category version of the variable is as follows:

	Hotels	*Respondents*
Low (5–8)	9	67
Medium (9)	8	96
High (10–11)	4	42
	21	205

THE AGGRESSION OF TOP MANAGEMENT

We define this variable as the mean score of top management on the aggression index. The following are the marginals for hotels and for respondents on a four-category version of the variable.

	Hotels	*Respondents*
Low (1–5)	7	54
Medium-Low (6–7)	6	62
Medium-High (9)	5	43
High (11)	3	46
	21	205

THE ABASEMENT OF TOP MANAGEMENT

This is defined as the mean abasement score of the two leading executives. The marginals for hotels and respondents on a trichotomized version are:

	Hotels	*Respondents*
Low (2–4)	6	65
Medium (5–7)	8	67
High (8–10)	7	73
	21	205

TOP MANAGEMENT'S NEED FOR SOCIAL APPROVAL

This is the mean score of the leading two executives on the index of the need for social approval. Hotels and respondents are distributed on this variable in the following manner:

	Hotels	*Respondents*
Low (3–6)	5	88
Medium (7–10)	7	68
High (11–19)	9	49
	21	205

THE SYMPATHY OF TOP MANAGEMENT

This variable is defined as the mean score of top management on the index of sympathy. The distribution of hotels and respondents follows:

	Hotels	*Respondents*
Low (1–5)	4	56
Medium (6–8)	10	88
High (9–12)	7	61
	21	205

Bibliography

Books

ANGELL, R. C. *Free Society and Moral Crisis.* Ann Arbor: University of Michigan Press, 1958.

———. *The Moral Integration of American Cities.* Chicago: University of Chicago Press, 1951.

BANDURA, A., and WALTERS, R. H. *Adolescent Aggression: A Study of the Influence of Child-Training Practices and Family Interrelationships.* New York: Ronald Press, 1959.

BERKOWITZ, LEONARD. *The Development of Motives and Values in the Child.* New York: Basic Books, 1964.

BLAU, PETER M., and SCOTT, W. RICHARD. *Formal Organizations: A Comparative Approach.* San Francisco: Chandler Publishing Company, 1962. Chapter 6.

BOTT, E. *Family and Social Network.* London: Tavistock Publications, 1957.

COOLEY, C. H. *Human Nature and the Social Order.* In *The Two Major Works of Charles H. Cooley.* Glencoe: The Free Press, 1956.

DE GRAZIA, S. *The Political Community: A Study of Anomie.* Chicago: University of Chicago Press, 1948.

EDWARDS, A. L. *Manual for the Edwards Personal Preference Schedule.* New York: Psychological Corporation, 1959.

———. *The Social Desirability Variable in Personality Assessment and Research.* New York: The Dryden Press, 1957.

ETZIONI, A. *A Comparative Study of Complex Organizations.* New York: The Free Press, 1961. Pp. 127–37.

FREUD, S. *An Autobiographical Study.* In J. Strachey, trans. and ed., *The Standard Edition of the Complete Psychological Works of Sigmund Freud.* Vol. 20. London: Hogarth Press, 1961.

———. *Civilization and Its Discontents.* New York: W. W. Norton and Company, 1962.

———. *The Ego and the Id.* In J. Strachey, trans. and ed., *The Standard Edition of the Complete Psychological Works of Sigmund Freud.* Vol 19. London: Hogarth Press, 1961.

———. *New Introductory Lectures on Psychoanalysis.* New York: W. W. Norton, 1933.

FUNKENSTEIN, D. H.; KING, S. H.; and DROLETTE, M. E. *Mastery of Stress.* Cambridge, Mass.: Harvard University Press, 1957.

GLUECK, S., and GLUECK, E. *Unraveling Juvenile Delinquency.* Cambridge, Mass.: Harvard University Press for the Commonwealth Fund, 1950.

GOLDSEN, R. K., et al. *What College Students Think.* Princeton, N.J.: D. Van Nostrand Company, 1960.

GROSS, N.; MASON, W. S.; and MCEACHERN, A. W. *Explorations in Role Analysis.* New York: John Wiley and Sons, 1958.

GUILFORD, J. P. *Personality.* New York: McGraw-Hill, 1959.

HARE, A. PAUL. *Handbook of Small Group Research.* New York: The Free Press, 1962.

HARRIS, KERR, FORSTER, AND COMPANY. *Trends in the Hotel Business, 1961.* 26th Annual Review. New York.

HARTSHORNE, H., and MAY, M. A. *Studies in the Nature of Character: I. Studies in Deceit.* New York: Macmillan, 1928.

HENRY, JULES. *Culture Against Man.* New York: Random House, 1963.

HORWATH and HORWATH. *Hotel Operations in 1961.* 30th Annual Study. New York, 1962.

JONES, E. *Sigmund Freud: Life and Work.* Vol. 3: *The Last Phase, 1919–1939.* London: Hogarth Press, 1957.

———. *The Life and Work of Sigmund Freud.* Edited and abridged by L. Trilling and S. Marcus. Garden City, N.Y.: Anchor Books, 1963.

LANDER, B. *Towards an Understanding of Juvenile Delinquency.* New York: Columbia University Press, 1954.

LATTIN, G. W. *Modern Hotel Management.* San Francisco: W. H. Freeman and Company, 1958.

MACIVER, R. M. *The Ramparts We Guard.* New York: Macmillian, 1950.

MEAD, G. H. *The Social Psychology of George Herbert Mead.* Edited by A. Strauss. Chicago: University of Chicago Press, 1956.

PECK, R. F., and HAVIGHURST, R. J. *The Psychology of Character Development.* New York: John Wiley, 1960.

PRESTHUS, R. *The Organizational Society.* New York: Knopf, 1962.

PUNER, H. W. *Freud: His Life and Mind.* New York: Dell Publishing Company, 1961.

SCHUTZ, W. C. *FIRO: A Three-Dimensional Theory of Interpersonal Behavior.* New York: Rinehart, 1958.

SEARS, R. R.; MACCOBY, E. E.; and LEVIN, H. *Patterns of Child Rearing.* Evanston, Illinois: Row, Peterson, 1957.

SEARS, R. R., et al. *Identification and Child Rearing*. London: Tavistock Publications, 1966.

SOROKIN, P. A. *Altruistic Love*. Boston: Beacon Press, 1950.

———. *Social and Cultural Mobility*. Glencoe, Ill.: Free Press, 1959.

———. *Social and Cultural Dynamics*. Vol. 3. New York: American Book Company, 1937.

SUTHERLAND, E. H. *White Collar Crime*. New York: Dryden Press, 1949.

TOENNIES, F. *Community and Society*. Translated by C. P. Loomis. East Lansing: Michigan State University Press, 1957.

U.S. Department of Labor, Bureau of Labor Statistics. *Employment Outlook in Hotel Occupations*. Occupational Outlook Series, Bulletin no. 905. Washington, D.C.: Government Printing Office, 1947.

WHITING, J. W. M., and CHILD, I. L. *Child Training and Personality*. New Haven: Yale University Press, 1953.

Articles

ADAMS, B. N. "Interaction Theory and Social Network." *Sociometry* 30 (1967):64–78.

ALLEN, R. M. "The Relationship Between the Edwards Personal Preference Schedule Variables and the Minnesota Multiphasic Personality Inventory Scales." *Journal of Applied Psychology* 41 (1957):307–11.

ALLINSMITH, W. "Moral Standards: II. The Learning of Moral Standards." In *Inner Conflict and Defense*, edited by D. R. Miller and G. E. Swanson, pp. 141–76. New York: Holt, 1960.

——— and GREENING, T. C. "Guilt Over Anger as Predicted from Parental Discipline: A Study of Superego Development." *American Psychologist* 10 (1955):320 (abstract).

AXELROD, M. "Urban Structure and Social Participation." *American Sociological Review* 21 (1956):13–18.

BAKER, B. O., and SARBIN, T. R. "Differential Mediation of Social Perception as a Correlate of Social Adjustment." *Sociometry* 19 (1956): 69–83.

BANDURA, A., and MCDONALD, F. J. "The Influence of Social Reinforcement and the Behavior of Models in Shaping Children's Moral Judgments." *Journal of Abnormal and Social Psychology* 67 (1963): 274–82.

BARDIS, PANOS D. "A Comparative Study of Familism." *Rural Sociology* 24:362–71.

BARKLEY, K. L. "Development of the Moral Judgment of College Students." *Character and Personality* 10 (1942):199–212.

BELL, G. B., and HALL, H. E., JR. "The Relationship Between Leadership and Empathy." *Journal of Abnormal and Social Psychology* 49 (1954):156–57.

BELL, W. "Anomie, Social Isolation, and the Class Structure." *Sociometry* 20 (1957): 105–16.

———. "Social Choice, Life Style and Suburban Residence." In *The Suburban Community*, edited by W. M. Dobriner, pp. 225–47. New York: Putnam, 1958.

——— and BOAT, M. T. "Urban Neighborhoods and Informal Social Relations." *American Journal of Sociology* 62 (1957): 391–98.

BORISLOW, B. "Edwards Personal Preference Schedule and Fakability." *Journal of Applied Psychology* 42 (1958): 22–27.

BORNSTON, F. L., and COLEMAN, J. C. "The Relationship Between Certain Parents' Attitudes Toward Child Rearing and the Direction of Aggression of Their Young Adult Offspring." *Journal of Clinical Psychology* 12 (1956): 41–44.

BRONFENBRENNER, U. "The Role of Age, Sex, Class, and Culture in Studies of Moral Development." *Religious Education* 57 (1962): Research Supplement, 3–17.

———. "Toward a Theoretical Model for the Analysis of Parent-Child Relationships in a Social Context." In J. C. Glidewell, *Parental Attitudes and Child Behavior*, pp. 90–109. Springfield, Ill.: Thomas, 1961.

——— et al. "The Measurement of Skill in Social Perception." In *Talent and Society*, edited by D. McClelland, et al., pp. 29–108. Princeton, N.J.: Van Nostrand and Company, 1958.

BROWN, A. W., et al. "Influence of Affectional Family Relationships on Character Development." *Journal of Abnormal and Social Psychology* 42 (1947): 422–28.

BUCHHEIMER, A. "The Development of Ideas About Empathy." *Journal of Counseling Psychology* 10 (1963): 61–70.

BURTON, R. V., et al. "Antecedents of Resistance to Temptation in Four-Year-Old Children." *Child Development* 32 (1961): 689–710.

CAMERON, N. "Paranoid Conditions and Paranoia." In *American Handbook of Psychiatry*, edited by S. Arieti. New York: Basic Books, 1959.

CAMPBELL, E. Q. "The Internalization of Moral Norms." *Sociometry* 27 (1964): 391–412.

CATTELL, R. B., et al. "The Dimensions of Syntality in Small Groups: I. The Neonate Group." *Human Relations* 6 (1953): 331–56.

CHANCE, J. E., and Meaders, W. "Needs and Interpersonal Perception." *Journal of Personality* 28 (1960): 200–09.

CLECKLEY, H. M. "Psychopathic States." In *American Handbook of Psychiatry*, edited by S. Arieti. New York: Basic Books, 1959.

CLOWARD, R. A. "Illegitimate Means, Anomie, and Deviant Behavior." *American Sociological Review* 24 (1959): 164–76.

COHEN, Y. A. "Food and Its Vicissitudes: A Cross-Cultural Study of Sharing and Nonsharing." In *Social Structure and Personality*, edited by Y. A. Cohen, pp. 312–46. New York: Holt, Rinehart and Winston, 1961.

———. "Patterns of Friendship." In *Social Structure and Personality*, edited by Y. A. Cohen, pp. 351–82. New York: Holt, Rinehart and Winston, 1961.

COLEMAN, J. S. "Relational Analysis: The Study of Social Organizations with Survey Methods." *Human Organization* 17 (Winter, 1958–59): 29–36.

COTTRELL, L. S., JR., and DYMOND, R. I. "The Empathic Responses." *Psychiatry* 12 (1949): 355–59.

COUCH, A., and KENISTON, K. "Agreeing Response Set and Social Desirability." *Journal of Abnormal and Social Psychology* 62 (1961): 175–79.

———. "Yeasayers and Naysayers: Agreeing Response Set as a Personality Variable." *Journal of Abnormal and Social Psychology* 60 (1960): 151–74.

CRONBACH, L. J. "Processes Affecting Scores on 'Understanding of Others' and 'Assumed Similarity.'" *Psychological Bulletin* 52 (1955): 177–93.

DANIELIAN, J. "Psychological and Methodological Evaluation of the Components of Judging Accuracy." *Perceptual and Motor Skills* 24 (1967): 1155–69.

DAVOL, S. H., and Reimanis, G. "The Role of Anomie as a Psychological Concept." *Journal of Individual Psychology* 15 (1959): 215–25.

DOTSON, F. "Patterns of Voluntary Association Among Urban Working-Class Families." *American Sociological Review* 16 (1951): 689–93.

DUBIN, R. "Deviant Behavior and Social Structure: Continuities in Social Theory." *American Sociological Review* 24 (1959): 147–64.

DUNNETTE, M. D., et al. "Relations Among Scores on Edwards Personal Preference Schedule, California Psychological Inventory, and Strong Vocational Interest Blank for an Industrial Sample." *Journal of Applied Psychology* 42 (1958): 178–81.

DYMOND, R. F. "A Preliminary Investigation of the Relation of Insight and Empathy." *Journal of Consulting Psychology* 12 (1948): 228–33.

———. "A Scale for the Measurement of Empathic Ability." *Journal of Consulting Psychology* 13 (1949): 127–33.

DYNES, R., et al. "Levels of Occupational Aspiration: Some Aspects of Family Experience as a Variable." *American Sociological Review* 21 (1956): 212–15.

EDWARDS, A. L. "Social Desirability or Acquiescence in the MMPI? A Case Study with the SD Scale." *Journal of Abnormal and Social Psychology* 63 (1961): 351–59.

——— and WALKER, J. N. "A Note on the Couch and Keniston Measure of Agreement Response Set." *Journal of Abnormal and Social Psychology* 62 (1961): 173–74.

———. "Social Desirability and Agreement Response Set." *Journal of Abnormal and Social Psychology* 62 (1961): 180–83.

——— et al. "A Note on Social Desirability as a Variable in the Edwards Personal Preference Schedule." *Journal of Consulting Psychology* 23 (1959): 558.

ERIKSEN, C. W. "Some Implications for TAT Interpretations Arising from Need and Perception Experiments." *Journal of Personality* 19 (1950): 282–88.

FAVA, S. F. "Contrasts in Neighboring: New York City and a Suburban County." In *The Suburban Community*, edited by W. M. Dobriner, pp. 122–31. New York: Putnam, 1958.

———. "Suburbanism as a Way of Life." *American Sociological Review* 21 (1956): 34–37.

FOURIEZAS, N., et al. "Measurement of Self-Oriented Needs in Discussion Groups." *Journal of Abnormal and Social Psychology* 45 (1950): 682–90.

FRITZ, M. F. "Relation of the Fritz-Neidt Practical Policy Test to Freshman Entrance Tests." *Proceedings of the Iowa Academy of Science* 57 (1950):379–80.

———. "A Short-Form Test of Cynicism." *Proceedings of the Iowa Academy of Science* 55 (1948):319–22.

———. "A Test Study of Cynicism and Idealism." *Proceedings of the Iowa Academy of Science* 53 (1946):269–72.

GAGE, N. L., and CRONBACH, L. J. "Conceptual and Methodological Problems in Interpersonal Perception." *Psychological Review* 62 (1955):411–22.

GLAZER, D. "A Note on 'Differential Mediation of Social Perception as a Correlate of Social Adjustment.'" *Sociometry* 20 (1957):156–60.

GOODE, W. J. "Illegitimacy, Anomie, and Cultural Penetration." *American Sociological Review* 26 (1961):910–25.

———. "Norm Commitment and Conformity to Role-Status Obligation." *American Journal of Sociology* 66 (1960): 246–58.

GORDON, LEONARD V. "Validities of the Forced-Choice and Questionnaire Methods of Personality Measurement." *Journal of Applied Psychology* 35 (1951):407–12.

GOUGH, H. G. "A Sociological Theory of Psychopathy." *American Journal of Sociology* 53 (1948):359–66.

———. "Theory and Measurement of Socialization." In *Studies in Behavior Pathology*, edited by T. R. Sarbin. New York: Holt, Rinehart and Winston, 1961. Pp. 141–49.

——— and PETERSON, D. R. "The Identification of and Measurement of Predispositional Factors in Crime and Delinquency." *Journal of Consulting Psychology* 16 (1952):207–12.

GREER, S. "Urbanism Reconsidered: A Comparative Study of Local Areas in a Metropolis." *American Sociological Review* 21 (1956): 19–25.

——— and KUBE, E. "Urbanism and Social Structure: A Los Angeles Study." In *Community Structure and Analysis*, edited by M. B. Sussman. New York: Thomas Y. Crowell, 1959.

GRINDER, R. E. "Parental Childrearing Practices, Conscience, and Resistance to Temptation of Sixth Grade Children." *Child Development* 33 (1962):803–20.

GUILFORD, J. P., and ZIMMERMAN, W. S. "Fourteen Dimensions of Temperament." *Psychological Monographs* 70 (1956), no. 417.

HALL, R. L. "Social Influence on the Aircraft Commander's Role." *American Sociological Review* 20 (1955):294–99.

HASTORF, A. H., and BENDER, I. E. "A Caution Respecting Measurement of Empathic Ability." *Journal of Abnormal and Social Psychology* 47 (1952):574–76.

HATHAWAY, S. R. "Rural-Urban Adolescent Personality." *Rural Sociology* 24 (1959):331–46.

HAYTHORN, W. "The Influence of Individual Members on the Characteristics of Small Groups." *Journal of Abnormal and Social Psychology* 48 (1953):276–84.

——— et al. "The Effects of Varying Combinations of Authoritarian and Equalitarian Groups and Followers." *Journal of Abnormal and Social Psychology* 53 (1956):210–19.

HEILBRUN, A. B., and GOODSTEIN, L. D. "The Relationships Between Individually Defined and Group Defined Social Desirability and Performance on the Edwards Personal Preference Schedule." *Journal of Consulting Psychology* 25 (1961): 200–204.

———. "Social Desirability Response Set: Error or Predictor Variable." *Journal of Psychology* 51 (1961):321–29.

HEINEMAN, C. E. "A Forced-Choice Form of the Taylor Anxiety Scale." *Journal of Consulting Psychology* 17 (1953):447–54.

HILL, W. F. "Learning Theory and the Acquisition of Values." *Psychological Review* 67 (1960):317–31.

HOFFMAN, M. L. "Homogeneity of Member Personality and Its Effect on Group Problem-Solving." *Journal of Abnormal and Social Psychology* 58 (1959):27–32.

———. "Power Assertion by the Parent and Its Impact on the Child." *Child Development* 31 (1960):129–43.

———. "The Role of the Parent in the Child's Moral Growth." *Religious Education* 57 (1962): Research Supplement, 18–33.

——— and SALTZSTEIN, H. D. "Parent Discipline and the Child's Moral Development." *Journal of Personality and Social Psychology* 5 (1967):45–57.

HOILENBERG, E., and SPERRY, M. "Some Antecedents of Aggression and Effects of Frustration in Doll Play." *Personality* 1 (1951):32–43.

JACKSON, D. N., and MESSICK, S. J. "Content and Style in Personality Assessment." *Psychological Bulletin* 55 (1958):243–52.

JONASSEN, C. T. "Community Typology." In *Community Structure and Analysis*, edited by M. B. Sussman, pp. 15–36. New York: Thomas Y. Crowell, 1959.

JONES, E. E., and DAUGHERTY, B. N. "Political Orientation and the Perceptual Effects of an Anticipated Interaction." *Journal of Abnormal and Social Psychology* 59 (1959):340–49.

——— et al. "Some Determinants of Reactions to Being Approved or Disapproved as a Person." *Psychological Monographs* 76 (1962), no. 521.

JONES, V. "Character Development in Children—An Objective Approach." In *Manual of Child Psychology*, edited by L. Carmichael, pp. 707–51. New York: Wiley, 1946.

KAGEN, J., and MOSS, H. "The Stability of Passive and Dependent Behavior From Childhood Through Adulthood." *Childhood Development* 31 (1960): 577–91.

KILLIAN, L. M., and GRIGG, C. M. "Urbanism, Race, and Anomie." *American Journal of Sociology* 67 (1962): 661–65.

LESSER, G. S. "The Relationship Between Overt and Fantasy Aggression as a Function of Maternal Response to Aggression." *Journal of Abnormal and Social Psychology* 55 (1957):218–21.

LEVONIAN, E., et al. "A Statistical Evaluation of Edwards Personal Preference Schedule." *Journal of Applied Psychology* 43 (1959):355–59.

LOCKE, H. J. "Mobility and Family Disorganization." *American Sociological Review* 5 (1940):489–94.

LYKKEN, D. T. "A Study of Anxiety in the Sociopathic Personality." In *Studies in Behavior Pathology*, edited by T. R. Sarbin, pp. 149–54. New York: Holt, Rinehart and Winston, 1961.

MCCORD, W.; MCCORD, J.; and HOWARD, A. "Familial Correlates of Aggression in Nondelinquent Male Children." *Journal of Abnormal and Social Psychology* 62 (1961): 79–93.

MARKS, E., and LINDSAY, C. A. "Machiavellian Attitudes: Some Measurement and Behavioral Considerations." *Sociometry* 29 (1966):228–36.

MARQUIS, D., et al. "A Social Psychological Study of the Decision-Making Conference." In *Groups, Leadership, and Men*, edited by H. Guetzkow, pp. 55–67. Pittsburgh: Carnegie Press, 1951.

MARWELL, G. "Problems of Operational Definitions of 'Empathy,' 'Identification,' and Related Concepts." *Journal of Social Psychology* 63 (1964): 87–102.

MEDALIA, N. Z. "Authoritarianism, Leader Acceptance and Group Cohesion." *Journal of Abnormal and Social Psychology* 51 (1955):207–13.

MEIER, DOROTHY L., and BELL, W. "Anomia and Differential Access to the Achievement of Life Goals." *American Sociological Review* 24 (1959):189–202.

MERRILL, R. M. and HEATHERS, L. B. "The Relation of the MMPI to the Edwards Personal Preference Schedule on a College Counseling Center Sample." *Journal of Consulting Psychology* 20 (1956):310–14.

MERTON, R. K. "Continuities in the Theory of Social Structure and Anomie." In *Social Theory and Social Structure*. Rev. ed., pp. 161–94. Glencoe, Ill.: Free Press, 1957.

———. "Social Conformity, Deviation, and Opportunity Structures: A Comment on the Contributions of Dubin and Cloward." *American Sociological Review* 24 (1959):177–89.

———. "Social Structure and Anomie." In *Social Theory and Social Structure*. Rev. ed., pp. 131–60. Glencoe, Ill.: Free Press, 1957.

MICHAELS, J. J. "Character Structure and Character Disorders." In *American Handbook of Psychiatry*, edited by S. Arieti. New York: Basic Books, 1959.

MIZRUCHI, E. H. "Social Structure and Anomia." *American Sociological Review* 25 (1960):645–54.

MURRAY, H. A. "The Effect of Fear Upon Estimates of the Maliciousness of Other Personalities." *Journal of Social Psychology* 4 (1933):310–29.

NEIDT, C. O. "Relation of Cynicism to Certain Other Variables." *Proceedings of the Iowa Academy of Science* 53 (1946):277–83.

———. "Selection of the Optimal Scoring Plan for the Fritz Test of Cynicism." *Proceedings of the Iowa Academy of Science* 54 (1947):253–62.

——— and FRITZ, M. F. "Relation of Cynicism to Certain Student Characteristics." *Educational and Psychological Measurement* 10 (1950):212–17.

NEIMAN, L. J., and HUGHES, J. W. "The Problem of the Concept of Role: A Resurvey of the Literature." *Social Forces* 30 (1951):141–49.

NETTLER, G. "Antisocial Sentiment and Criminality." *American Sociological Review* 24 (1959):202–8.

NEWCOMB, T. M. "The Study of Consensus." In *Sociology Today: Problems and Prospects*, edited by R. K. Merton, et al., pp. 277–92. New York: Basic Books, 1959.

OSBURN, H. G., et al. "The Relative Validity of Forced Choice and Single Stimulus Self Description Items." *Educational and Psychological Measurement* 14 (1954): 407–17.

POSTMAN, L., BRUNER, J. S., and MCGINNIES, E. "Personal Values as Selective Factors in Perception." *Journal of Abnormal and Social Psychology* 43 (1948): 142–54.

RAMSAY, R. W., et al. "Conscience Operation in a Normal Population." *Journal of the Canadian Psychiatric Association* 11 (1966):80–90.

RECKLESS, W. C., et al. "The 'Good' Boy in a High Delinquency Area." *Journal of Criminal Law and Criminology* 48 (1957):18–25.

ROBERTS, A. H., and ROKEACH, M. "Anomie, Authoritarianism, and Prejudice: A Replication." *American Journal of Sociology* 61 (1956):355–58.

SANFORD, F. H. "The Follower's Role in Leadership Phenomena." In *Readings in Social Psychology*, edited by G. E. Swanson, et al., rev. ed., pp. 328–40. New York: Henry Holt and Company, 1952.

SARBIN, T. R., and BAKER, B. O. "Psychological Predisposition and/or Subcultural Participation." *Sociometry* 20 (1957):161–64.

SCHUTZ, W. C. "What Makes Groups Productive?" *Human Relations* 8 (1955): 429–65.

SEARS, R. R. "The Growth of Conscience." In *Personality Development in Children*, edited by I. Iscoe and H. W. Stevenson. Austin: University of Texas Press, 1960.

——— et al. "Some Child-Rearing Antecedents of Aggression and Dependency in Young Children." *Genetic Psychology Monographs* 47 (1953):135–236.

SMITH, C. G. "A Comparative Analysis of Some Conditions and Consequences of Intra-Organizational Conflict." *Administrative Science Quarterly* 10 (1966): 504–29.

SMITH, J., et al. "Local Intimacy in a Middle-Sized City." *American Journal of Sociology* 60 (1954):277–83.

SROLE, L. "Social Integration and Certain Corollaries: An Exploratory Study." *American Sociological Review* 21 (1956):709–16.

STEINER, I. D. "Interpersonal Behavior as Influenced by Accuracy of Social Perception." In *Current Perspectives in Social Psychology*, edited by E. P. Hollander and R. G. Hunt. 2d ed., pp. 266–71. New York: Oxford University Press, 1967.

STOGDILL, R. M. "Personal Factors Associated with Leadership: A Survey of the Literature." *Journal of Psychology* 25 (1948):35–71.

STRACHEY, J. Editor's Introduction to *The Ego and the Id*, by S. Freud. In *The Standard Edition of the Complete Psychological Works of Sigmund Freud*. Translated and edited by J. Strachey. Vol. 19, pp. 3–11. London: Hogarth Press, 1961.

STRYKER, S. "Role-Taking Accuracy and Adjustment." In *Sourcebook in Marriage and the Family*, edited by M. B. Sussman. 2d ed., pp. 385–93. Boston: Houghton Mifflin, 1963.

TAFT, R. "The Ability to Judge People." *Psychological Bulletin* 52 (1955): 1–23.

TAYLOR, J. Z. "The 'Yeasayer' and Social Desirability: A Comment on the Couch and Keniston Paper." *Journal of Abnormal and Social Psychology* 62 (1961): 172.

THOMAS, E. J. "Role Conceptions and Organizational Size." *American Sociological Review* 24 (1959):30–37.

TOLOR, A. "The Relationship Between Insight and Intraception." *Journal of Clinical Psychology* 17 (1961):188–89.

——— and REZNIKOFF, M. "A New Approach to Insight: A Preliminary Report." *Journal of Nervous and Mental Disease* 130 (1960):286–96.

TURNER, R. H. "Role-Taking, Role Standpoint and Reference Group Behavior." *American Journal of Sociology* 61 (1956):316–28.

USEEM, R. H., et al. "The Function of Neighboring for the Middle Class Male." *Human Organization* 19 (1960):68–76.

WALLIN, P. "A Guttman Scale for Measuring Woman's Neighborliness." *American Journal of Sociology* 59 (1953):243–46.

WEEKS, H. A. "Male and Female Broken Home Rates by Types of Delinquency." *American Sociological Review* 5 (1940):601–9.

WHITE, R., and LIPPITT, R. "Leader Behavior and Member Reaction in Three 'Social Climates.'" In *Group Dynamics: Research and Theory*, edited by D. Cartwright and A. Zander. 2d ed., pp. 527–54. Evanston, Ill.: Row, Peterson and Company, 1960.

WILLIAMS, R. M., JR. "Friendship and Social Values in a Suburban Community: An Exploratory Study." *Pacific Sociological Review* 2 (1959):3–10.

WILLIAMSON, R. C. "Socio-Economic Factors and Marital Adjustment in an Urban Setting." *American Sociological Review* 19 (1954):213–16.

WRIGHT, B. A. "Altruism in Children and the Perceived Conduct of Others." *Journal of Abnormal and Social Psychology* 37 (1942):218–33.

ZUCKERMAN, M. "The Validity of the Edwards Personal Preference Schedule in the Measurement of Dependency-Rebelliousness." *Journal of Clinical Psychology* 14 (1958):379–82.

ZETTERBERG, H. L. "Compliant Actions." *Acta Sociologica* 2 (1957):179–201.

Unpublished Sources

CHRISTIE, R. "Impersonal Interpersonal Orientations and Behavior." Research proposal submitted to the Division of Social Sciences, National Science Foundation. Mimeographed. New York: Columbia University, 1962.

DYMOND, R. F. "Empathic Ability: An Exploratory Study." Ph.D. dissertation, Cornell University, 1949.

SLATER, P. E. "Psychological Factors in Role Specialization." Ph.D. dissertation, Harvard University, 1955.

Index